A Stranger in My Land

by Sabra Holbrook

Sir Tristan of All Time
A Stranger in My Land

A Stranger in
My Land

A Life of
François Villon

Sabra Holbrook

Farrar, Straus and Giroux
New York

4/28 23

Copyright © 1972 by Sabra Holbrook

First printing, 1972

Library of Congress catalog card number: 76-184702
ISBN 0-374-37276-4
Printed in the United States of America
Published simultaneously in Canada
by Doubleday Canada Ltd., Toronto
Designed by Sheila Lynch

Pour
JEAN CHRÉTIEN
Un fils de France, qui, lui aussi,
vit dans un siècle agité,
et qui, avec ses *Jeunes Agriculteurs,*
essaie de débarrasser son pays
des moeurs démodées, desséchées et étranglantes
pour y cultiver des voies à un futur épanoui
où il y aura des occasions fructueuses pour tous.

Contents

A Stranger in My Land

✢ CHAPTER I ✢

Confrontation

"Truly, no worse can be found than a student," groaned solid citizens. Their groan was the refrain of the Establishment, an Establishment outraged by the freakish, sometimes lawless behavior of the students in the university that towered on the hill above the city.

Toward evening, city shopkeepers and homeowners shuttered their windows and fastened stout bars along the streets winding uphill. They feared roving packs of students, who, in eccentric costumes and, like as not, armed with homemade weapons, haunted the nights. The police guard, though strong, wasn't strong enough to cope alone with the marauders, so every able citizen was required to serve with the night patrol three weeks every year—unless he could purchase exemption by doing some favor.

From their hilltop, the students looked down on the civil Establishment with derision. The police they rated even lower than civilians; they called them pigs. Regularly the pigs beat up the students, and just as regularly the students beat up the pigs. Indeed, the students were in conflict with almost all institutions except their own. During the long war then dragging to a close, professors had joined students in opposing the government's stand. Ever since, claimed the university chancellor, the government had been trying to suppress academic freedom.

Tension between scholars and community led to debates, disputes, charges and countercharges. One winter's day, the police arrested forty students, who were consigned to the darkest, dankest cells of the city jail and scantily fed on bread and water. The grounds for the general arrest were that "no worse could be found than a student."

When written protests from the university were ignored, the chancellor set out to pay a personal call on the police guard commander. He was accompanied by eight hundred students who marched behind him in one hundred blocs of eight men each. None was armed.

The marchers waited outside while the chancellor talked with the police commander. He came out with good news: an immediate inquiry would separate bystanders from activists among the jailed students; the innocent would be released and the others moved into standard cells and fed regulation meals.

Cheering at this progress, the students headed homeward. As the last of them entered a long narrow street, they were set upon from behind by armed police. Far up front, the street's entrance to a boulevard was blocked by more police. It was an ambush.

"Kill!" ordered the captain in charge. The students ran

for their lives, cutting through the yards of houses along the street. A number of them, forgetting their disdain of the average citizen, banged on doors, seeking refuge inside. They were greeted with brandished clubs and shovels. One graduate student of theology saw a guard aim at the chancellor and leaped forward in time to give his own life for the chancellor's.

After this catastrophe the university was closed for more than a year. This was life at the Sorbonne—the first university founded in the Western world—and this was the unease of Paris in the spring of 1453. Among student troublemakers was one who had just been awarded his master's degree in the College of the Arts, François Villon. So synonymous with youthful revolt was Villon's name that *villonerie* became a catchword for disorder on Mont Sainte Geneviève, the Sorbonne hill.

But there was more than rebellion in the soul of this young activist. His rhymed commentaries on the turmoil and the people of his times, which he had already begun to compose, were to give him a life through all time of which he never dreamed. Unfortunately, the satirical work in verse which he wrote about some of the events leading to the shutdown of the Sorbonne perished, no one knows where. From references in his later verse we know that he called it *Le Roman du Pet-au-Diable,* and that it was inspired by a student-community fracas over a great rock nicknamed Pet-au-Diable, the Devil's Windbreak.

The Windbreak sheltered the house of one Mademoiselle de Bruyères, a sanctimonious lady as well known for her determination to reform the prostitutes of Paris as for her colossal mistakes in identifying them. She raised a particular furor when she carried her campaign into the Marché au Fillé, the linen weavers' market. Its stalls were staffed by young girls with exemplary reputations, a qualification required ever since the market had been founded by Saint Louis, a revered and pious French monarch of the thirteenth century. As a double check on tradition, the stall girls worked under the watchful eyes of no-nonsense matrons.

In ironic verses which have survived, Villon suggested that Mademoiselle de Bruyères, having misdirected sufficient zeal into the Marché au Fillé, should henceforth address her sermons elsewhere—preferably to cemeteries. To outtalk the live and nimble-tongued Parisienne, he declared, she would need more fluency than the Apostles of Christ. So saying, he swung into the *Ballade of the Women of Paris*, which he dedicated to the Marché's stall girls, chattering at their work.

> Quoy qu'on tient belles langagieres
> Florentines, Veniciennes,
> Assez pour estre messaigieres,
> Et mesmement les anciennes;
> Mais, soient Lombardes, Rommaines,
> Genevoyses, à mes perilz,
> Piemontoises, Savoysiennes,
> Il n'est bon bec que de Paris.

De beau parler tiennent chayeres,
Ce dit-on, Neapolitaines,
Et que sont bonnes caquetieres
Allemandes et Prussiennes;
Soient Grecques, Egyptiennes,
De Hongrie ou d'autre pays,
Espaignolles ou Castellennes,
Il n'est bon bec que de Paris.

Brettes, Suysses, n'y sçavent gueres,
Ne Gasconnes et Thoulouzaines;
Du Petit-Pont deux harangeres
Les concluront, et les Lorraines,
Angloises ou Calaisiennes
(Ay-je beaucoup de lieux compris?)
Picardes, de Valenciennes;
Il n'est bon bec que de Paris.

Envoi

Prince, aux dames Parisiennes,
De bien parler donnez le prix;
Quoy qu'on die d'Italiennes,
Il n'est bon bec que de Paris.

I'll wager not on stranger's tongue,
Though fluent Florentine she be,
Or messenger with forceful lung,
Or character in history;
For whether Rome or Lombardy,
Venice or Genoa gave her wit,
Though from Savoy or Piedmont, she—
My Paris has the best of it.

Of Neapolitans it's sung
Their lasses would great preachers be,
While gossip scintillates among
The Prussian girls of Germany;
Irrelevant—nativity.
Hungarians, Greeks, Egyptians, quit—
And Catalans, admit you see
My Paris has the best of it.

You Bretons, Swiss, share bottom rung
With tongues from Toulouse, Gascony,
And those from Calais, England sprung,
Valence, Lorraine and Picardy;
(For oversights, please pardon me)
Two Paris vendors I would pit
Against the lot and guarantee
My Paris has the best of it.

Envoi

Milord, awards for fluency
The Paris women only fit.
Let the Italians disagree!
My Paris has the best of it.

The form of this poem, the ballade, had been developed
in France some one hundred years before Villon's time as
an appeal to nobles by poets in residence at royal courts.
After bolstering his case with rhymed argument, the poet
made his pitch in the *envoi,* the last four lines. The inflexible
discipline of the ballade, allowing only three or at most four

rhymes throughout, produced considerable awkwardness in the work of lesser poets than Villon. To him, constant rhyme was no problem. Often he burst into a ballade in the middle of other verses. Scholars who have specialized in the study of his work say that his *Ballade of the Women of Paris* probably first appeared as an interlude in his lost account of the affair of the Devil's Windbreak.

That affair, which was to end so tragically in ambush, began when Sorbonne students transferred the stone from the front yard of Mademoiselle de Bruyères to the courtyard of the Sorbonne. Mademoiselle, though quite unaware of the popular name for it, was very fond of this mass of rock which separated her house from the street. Indignantly, she informed the police of the theft. A cordon of them recovered the stone and dragged it to the courtyard of the Palais Royal, the chief seat of justice. There they held it for safekeeping while Mademoiselle had a substitute rock placed in front of her home.

About a year later, on a night just before the beginning of the Christmas holidays, a group of students known as Martinets, because of the *martins* or iron-tipped wooden batons which they carried, decided to reclaim the original stone from the Palais. Using crowbars, they forced up the Palais portcullis, a barrier of iron pikes normally raised or lowered by chains. They warned the porter inside to keep quiet. He did.

They found the stone in the middle of a courtyard surrounded by stalls of jewelers and vendors of embroidered silks, furs, books, games of checkers, dice, and the market's specialty: beautifully appareled dolls. At this season, not a little girl in Paris but begged Saint Nicholas for a Palais doll.

When the students arrived, dolls and other wares had been sold or put away for the night. The stalls were deserted, except for sleeping beggars. Empty also was the great hall into which the courtyard opened, where lawyers rented benches beneath gilded statues of the kings of France. The pickpockets who frequented the Palais daily had gone home, but the night life of the courtyard was in full swing. Prisoners from the Conciergerie, an annexed jail, were throwing dice, having bribed guards to let them out of their cells.

No doubt to the amusement of these prisoners, the students carried off the stone. Along the way the idea came to them to complete the job by lifting as well the replacement in front of Mademoiselle de Bruyères' house. They also unhinged various signs swinging above the doors of some of the shops and taverns they passed. From among such choices as the Antlered Cerf, the Shrimp, the Golden Sheep, the Crowned Bull, the Bound Cow, the Fat Sow, the Hungry Bear, and others, the students made a thoughtful selection. They had a plan for the use of particular ones.

If they sang as they climbed Mont Sainte Geneviève, their song might have been a favorite about a Paris beauty; no doubt their voices came on strong with the ditty's chorus, which another of Villon's verses quotes as "Open your door, Guillemette." Then, likely as not, some burgher disturbed from sleep called from his window *"Gare l'eau!"* "Watch out for the water!" and having delivered his warning, dumped bucketfuls on the heads of any not agile enough to have sidestepped his aim.

Hearing the rumpus, the *oublieurs,* sellers of little pastries who searched the night streets for customers, might well have hurried to the scene, crying, *"Oublie, oublie,"* steadying their pastry trays strapped over their shoulders. Students whose allowances permitted them to indulge their palates were among the *oublieurs'* best customers. Their love of sweets was rarely satisfied by the meager menus in the houses of the professors with whom they boarded. A generous student with a newly replenished purse might also buy for his friends and for the carolers who would have caught up with the goings-on.

So, perhaps munching as they sang, the students continued their climb, bearing their burdens of gilded signs and dragging the stolen stones in a homemade cart. Their mottled pony-skin shoes crunched the snow; the braid-trimmed hoods of their cloaks were pulled over their shaven heads against the cold and the possibility of a dunking from above. Like those of monks and priests, their heads were tonsured, that is to say shaven clean, except for a circular fringe of hair which many of them allowed to grow long in back. Their tunics, worn over snug tights, were considerably shorter than was considered decent. On the hands of those hauling the cart could be seen ten rings—one for each finger. The rings glittered in the light of candles set before shrines of saints at crossroads or in the glow of lanterns blinking from behind tavern windows.

Every so often, one group of haulers was relieved by another, and those who had finished their stint blew on their hands and buried them deep in their tunic pockets. It was cold. And dark. Except for occasional candles and lanterns, all lights had been extinguished with the 9 p.m. *couvre-feu,* the cover-fire or curfew, established to save scarce and costly fuel and to prevent fires. This was the *heure douteuse,* the hour of uncertainty when thieves crept about, a hungry wolf might howl, students roistered, and citizens who had not been able to avoid guard duty groped warily on patrol, hugging the buildings that lined the icy streets.

Villon had had his share of nights of bloody skirmishes with patrols, when he had ended up done in, as his verses recall, *à bas chevet,* with the ground for a pillow. This time there was no fight. The students marched on until they reached the Sorbonne, where they fastened the Pet-au-Diable with bands of steel to a pedestal which they plastered into the university courtyard. Nearby they placed Mademoiselle de Bruyères' substitute rock. They topped both rocks with wreaths of evergreen and then conducted with mock solemnity a marriage of the stolen signs. They wed the Fat Sow to the Hungry Bear, the Bound Cow to the Crowned

Bull, and so on until each sign had the mate the students considered appropriate. Then, exhausted, they went to bed.

At dawn watchmen in the towers of the Châtelet, the principal prison of Paris, and of the Louvre, the king's residence, wakened the populace with trumpet blasts. The bells in the twin towers of the Cathedral of Notre Dame— La Jacqueline, the biggest, and the softer sister bells— clanged in chorus. All over Paris, the bells of dozens more churches chimed. Daytime sounds replaced the cries of night. Anvils rang in blacksmiths' forges. Saws whined in carpenters' sheds. Copper melders' furnaces crackled.

The police guard went sleepily home. The captain sat down to write his report. It included the theft of the stones and signs, a theft soon traced to the Sorbonne. The commander of the guard threatened to recover the stolen property, despite the tradition which, in the name of academic freedom, prevented the police from setting foot in university precincts. "He won't dare," the students said of the commander's threat. "And if he does, there will be some broken guardsmen's heads." For several nights they held dances around the stones to the music of flutes and drums, forcing all who passed by to join their rites.

But the police commander had not been bluffing. Selecting a crack group of officers, he led them up Mont Sainte Geneviève. Near the university he stopped off in the home of a friend to enjoy a bit of wine while his officers raided house after house where students boarded with their professors. In one of these houses a small cannon and a collection of knives were found. Students had intended to use these if the police invaded, but the attack had been too sudden for them to organize their defense.

In another house, most of the stolen signs were located. The arms, the signs, the stones were hefted into a cart and packed off down the hill. The police then began a systematic looting of the neighborhood. The lieutenant in charge gave the orders: "Break up everything, take everything, and if anyone rebels, kill everyone." They stole dishes and silverware, tablecloths, textbooks, pots and pans, even the bedsheets. "To give them heart for this task," writes a chronicler of the time, "they did not deprive themselves of drinking the wine from the cellars of the professors." One tipsy sergeant, yanking a professor's robe from its hook, continued his uncertain progress with the flowing gown billowing over his uniform. To the community of scholars, this was perhaps the greatest sacrilege of all.

Before the raid was over, forty students had been seized, without regard to whether or not they had been involved in the Pet-au-Diable affair and without regard to whether or not they resisted the police invasion. These were the forty students whose arrest prompted the chancellor of the university to call on the police commander, accompanied by the eight hundred protesting students. After the ambush that followed and the closing of the university, the highest court in the land began an investigation of the whole conflict.

Though the government might be exasperated by the university, it dared not disregard it. The investigation resulted in the dismissal of the officers involved in the ambush. The investigators also ordered that the guard who had killed the theology student should have his right hand cut off. Mollified, the Sorbonne administrators reopened the university.

It was not the business of the court to delve into the depths of social discord of which student and police behavior alike were merely surface symptoms in mid-fifteen-century Paris, as in all France. François Villon, active participant in student-community confrontation, was born into the final throes of this discord. His life teetered on the descending end of a time seesaw; medieval France was declining; the France of the Renaissance was on its way up.

✢ CHAPTER II ✢

Dark Before Dawn

To understand Villon the man, and to appreciate Villon the poet, one must grope with him for a while through the half light of the fading fifteenth century. For six previous centuries men who earned their own living had been shackled to nobles who had inherited or seized wealth and estates. Whether the working man wove tapestries, grew vegetables, sculptured statues of saints for cathedrals, forged horseshoes, wrote ballades for dukes, or raised cattle—no matter. His social status differed, depending on his occupation, but his dependence on the whim of his liege lord did not.

This feudalism—this medieval system of organizing society from the top down—was beginning to fall apart by the time Villon and his fellow students at the Sorbonne were horrifying the solid citizens of Paris. War and disease had gnawed the population of the country in half over the previous hundred years. The bubonic plague and the Hundred Years' War between France and England had taken such brutal toll that survivors who possessed essential skills found themselves in great demand. They could safely desert their lords for the free market and sell to the highest bidder.

A sense of independence and with it a spirit of curiosity flowed from village marketplace to university classroom. In less than a century after Villon's day, these streams would swell to a refreshing torrent. They would lead to more sophisticated government; to the first modern ideas in geography, astronomy, and physics; to exploration of unknown continents, new forms of expression in art, architecture, and literature, new flexibility in man's approach to God. This was the coming Renaissance.

Meanwhile, almost everyone could feel some of feudalism's death pangs in a very sensitive area—the pocketbook. A free market meant higher prices. Furthermore, the continuous war, a vestige of rival feudal claims, was imposing a heavy tax burden. The roots of the war stretched far back to the seizure in 1066 of the throne of England by the French Duke of Normandy, William the Conqueror. Thereafter, William's descendants in England laid hereditary claim to varying portions of France. In 1154, William's great-grandson, Henry, residing in France, where he and his wife owned half the country, was crowned King of England. From that time on, English kings sought to wear the crown of both countries. In 1346, Henry's great-great-great-grandson, Edward III of England, invaded France, defeated the French with rapid-fire arrows from the newly invented English longbow, and declared himself King of England and France. Thus began the Hundred Years' War.

From time to time the resisting French threw the English out. But, decade after decade, they always returned. In 1422, nine years before Villon was born, a British duke ruled in Paris for an infant King of England and France. A substantial number of powerful French nobles, mainly in the duchy of Burgundy, had by then been won over to the support of the English. Siding with these Burgundians were certain groups of tradesmen—the butchers of Paris, for example—and certain enclaves of intellectuals, among them the professors and a majority of the students at the Sorbonne. The most prominent of the Burgundian sympathizers was the Queen of France herself. France was, in effect, in a state of civil war at home while trying to throw off aggression from abroad.

Taking advantage of the resulting chaos, packs of brigands roamed the country, many of them ex-soldiers discharged during lulls between critical periods of the war. Civil authority had broken down and destitution was such that many people were glad for a meal of apple or cabbage cores. When Villon was four years old, Paris was surrounded by Burgundians who slit the throat of any citizen seeking to leave the city. Two years later, when he was six, the Burgundians were replaced by an army of bandits who made forays into the city, along with the wolves. Hungry wolves and hungry bandits victimized equally hungry people.

One tailless wolf was caught. Parisians named him *Cour-*

tault, meaning bobtail. The expression *Gardez-vous de Courtault,* beware the bobtail, came to refer to wolves and thieves alike.

The winter that Courtault was caught, snow fell for forty days without stopping. High winds blew ceaselessly. A smallpox epidemic killed fifty thousand in Paris. But the hardy race of pickpockets, lockpickers, pilferers managed to survive. Those who died frozen *à bas chevet* were quickly replaced by others. Thieves were to be found even among the clergy. Many light-fingered youths became church clerks as a cover-up for their more lucrative careers. Should they be apprehended, they would be tried in a church court, notably more lenient than the civil courts. Non-clerical prisoners could sometimes bribe guards to bring them a church cassock and a razor for tonsuring their heads. They claimed the right to a church trial and often got away with their masquerade.

The slotted alms boxes in churches were special targets for thievery. Students, in particular, learned how to coat a length of rope with glue, poke it through the slot, swish it around, and withdraw it, coin-covered. This method of larceny had its own name: *prendre au glu,* literally to take with glue.

Prendre au glu was not, Villon thought, worth the risk. One of his childhood friends, René de Montigny, who, under the cover of church clerking, grew up to be the smoothest pickpocket of Paris, was finally hung for alms stealing. His net from that theft was paltry. "How truly witless," Villon wrote, "to risk body and soul for so little."

Life was fragile enough without taking foolish chances. The often-used gallows (nineteen of them); the nightly cries of the robbed and attacked; the howl of wolves and the horror of epidemics—these threw the shadow of death over all the days and nights of early-fifteenth-century Paris. Yet this was the city of Villon's heart. He wrote almost all his poetry in Paris, about Parisians. He was its voice. It was his inspiration. To find one's way around in his poetry, one has to know his Paris.

There is significance in the fact that in Villon's time one of the Parisians' favorite places to spend Sundays was the cemetery of the Church of the Innocents. Enclosed in walls ten feet thick, built by a fastidious nobleman to protect his own grave, the cemetery had become the graveyard of paupers. Sermons were preached there on Sundays, after which people shopped for books, yard goods, metalwork, and sweets in stalls erected on tombs and around the charnel houses. Where old graves had been churned up to make room for new bodies, customers had to kick scattered bones out of their way. On All Souls' Day, blind beggars squatted on the tombs, selling their prayers for a few coins. Beggars and vendors rented square footage from church wardens, some of whom were not above taking fees for the same space from two different tenants. Villon records a lively spat between a pastry maker and linen weaver to whom the same stall had been rented. Before the argument was settled, all the pastries and linens had been stolen.

In the walls of the church cloister reposed the rich dead. Under the cloister arches was a representation of the popular Danse Macabre, or Dance of the Dead, sometimes performed as part of church pageants. The musicians were skeletons. The dancers—popes, emperors, cardinals, kings, soldiers, priests, professors, monks, doctors, farmers, lovers, shoemakers, children—held rigid, motionless poses. Only one figure danced like mad. He was the figure of Death. The fresco represented his triumph over all. As Villon wrote:

> Quand je considere ces testes
> Entassees en ces charniers,
> Tous furent maistres des requestes,
> Au moins de la Chambre aux Deniers,
> Ou tous furent porte-paniers
> Autant puis l'ung que l'autre dire:
> Car, d'evesques ou lanterniers
> Je n'y congnois rien à dire.

> When I consider each poor head
> That here is left to gather mold,
> How this one as King's banker led
> A life that glowed with royal gold;
> And this one lugged through heat and cold
> His basketloads of clods and clay—
> No difference lasts when all is told,
> Archbishop, peasant, both decay.

During epidemics there was no promenading in the cemetery. Its three great gates were sealed in the hope of preventing the stench of decaying flesh from pervading the city. Corpses were brought in through an underground tunnel and buried rapidly, six hundred to a ditch. Since he lived in such times, it is small wonder that Villon's quatrain setting forth his identity and origin is devoted half and half to birth and death.

> Je suis François, dont il me poise
> Né de Paris emprès Pontoise;
> Et de la corde d'une toise
> Saura mon col que mon cul poise.

> I am François, which gives me pause
> Born in Paris, near Pontoise;
> Noosed in rope my neck shall fathom
> Alas, the last weight of my bottom.

Thirty years old when he wrote the quatrain, he was, according to his own description, bald, lacking eyebrows, with "teeth as widely separated as a rake's." A vivid scar from his upper lip to his nostrils was the souvenir of a knife duel with a priest. His slight body had the swollen stomach of malnutrition. It was further misshapen by arthritis developed in the damp of dungeons and perhaps also by the tortures applied to make prisoners confess or inform on accomplices. The most common of these was the *treteau*: hanging a man by the wrists while attaching increasing weights to his feet. At the age of thirty, Villon had been twice in jail and was in danger of a third term. He had good reason to fear the death on the gallows which, with typical Villonesque self-mockery, he described as his neck finding out what his bottom weighed.

He was born April 19, 1431, six weeks before nineteen-year-old Joan of Arc was burned alive by the Burgundians in Rouen. This uneducated teenager from the farmlands of Lorraine who declared that she was directed by the Saints of God had singlehandedly set in motion forces which finally drove the English forever from France. The end of the Hundred Years' War came during Villon's lifetime. A fervent patriot, Villon did not share university empathy with the Burgundians, or university views on the war. He cherished a profound admiration for Joan, whom he called "the holy girl of Lorraine." In a ballade to *Women of Days Gone By,* he equated her with those whom he considered history's greatest.

What a bundle of contrasts was this man, this poet, this philosopher and lawbreaker, this student clown, this keen observer! Born as the Middle Ages were dying, he is now considered the first of France's modern poets. A forerunner of the Renaissance in the realism of his subject matter, he was an agile master of the medieval ballade. Devout in his religion, he was often bitterly cynical toward the clergy. He mocked himself and wept for his world, railing against its inequalities:

> Et les aucuns sont devenuz
> Dieu mercy! grans seigneurs et maistres,
> Les autres mendient tous nudz
> Et pain ne voyent qu'aux fenestres . . .
>
> And some are nobles born to be
> Masters of all by God's strange grace,
> While others beg in nudity
> For bread locked in the baker's case . . .

Himself, he continues in this same poem, he is one of the beggars. To the rich, God has already given sufficient; "to the poor, who, like this writer, have nothing, God owes the gift of patience."

It was a gift François never received. He was impatient with the enemies of France, impatient with the women he desired and whom his ugliness repelled, impatient with the stolidity and frequent hypocrisy of the Establishment. His impatience drove him into the subculture of his city: the taverns of ill repute, the gambling games, the prostitutes, the slicksters, and finally crime.

Like many of his day, he sought refuge from the violence, the suffering, and the shadow of death around him in whatever enjoyments could be wrested from an escapade, a tankard too many of fine Beaune wine and the rare feeling of a comfortable bellyful after a good meal bought with stolen gold. And Paris, despite poverty, sieges, and smallpox, offered plenteous opportunity for such temporary escape from life's realities. Four thousand taverns—including Villon's favorite Pomme de Pin, the Pinecone—daily sold a hundred barrels of wine apiece. Hundreds more barrels were sold by householders who grew grapes in their back yards. Monasteries, convents, soldiers, all peddled wine. Sorbonne students often paid their professors for their board with wine produced from their parents' vineyards. Beaune, Villon's preference, was the most popular, but like other Parisians, he also enjoyed strong Burgundies: Saint Pourcain and Saint Jehan. These he liked best when mulled in a warm drink called Hypocras, to which freshly ground cinnamon, ginger, and pepper were added, with a flecking of sugar.

The taverns were not mere bars. They also served as convenient centers for transacting business. Over the wine, buyers and sellers sealed bargains, lawyers discussed settlement of cases, professors elected department chairmen. The hum of their conversation was punctuated by the rattle of dice, the click of billiards, the slapping of cards, the clatter of ninepins, and the bouncing of balls, as gamblers pushed their luck in games of chance.

Enterprising landowners often built tennis courts near taverns, for tennis, too, was played strictly for stakes. After paying up, the losers also had to buy the winners' drinks.

Rackets and balls were supplied by the court owner. Players were usually nude, for the owner held their clothes as security against lost balls and broken rackets. Understandably, tennis flourished only during the balmiest summer weeks.

In winter, before a great crackling hearth fire, a tavern meal was a treat to warm the cockles—and to deplete the purse. Should a man be too poor to afford such luxury, he could, if he had the right friends among servants of the rich, dine and wine lavishly for nothing. While many a master and mistress slept, their servants entertained in the kitchen. They didn't hesitate to open the best bottles from the wine cellar and serve the finest delicacies from the larder. "They think nothing of offering six or seven pints," Villon recorded in a lip-smacking stanza, "along with many pies, custards, and frothy cheese pastry."

Many of the chambermaids in such houses led a second life as prostitutes. In Villon's Paris, three thousand known prostitutes competed with each other. There were no houses of prostitution; the business was highly individual. Any female who judged herself qualified to succeed in it simply paid a fee to the commander of the police guard, whom the prostitutes regarded as their patron. Thereafter, she was on her own, safe from restriction or arrest.

These prostitutes, or, in language of the day, daughters of joy, or tarts, paraded in apparel worthy of queens. They wore rich but never gaudy clothes; flowing silken gowns with satin-lined sleeves, girdled at the waist with jeweled belts. The sole mark of their trade was a scarlet hood. On Sundays, they swished into church pews, carrying outsize prayer books which few of them could read. They adopted fanciful pseudonyms: la Chandelière aux Talons Courts, the Candlemaker with Short Heels; la Belle Cadranière, the Beautiful Sundial-maker; la Grande Hallebardière, the Great Halberd-maker.

La Belle Heaulmière, the Beautiful Helmet-maker, was the most famous of them all. One of Villon's ballades purports to be a lecture which la Belle Heaulmière is giving six sister prostitutes—the beautiful glove-maker, the gentle sausage-maker, the purse-maker, the cobbler, the rug-maker, and the hood-maker. The theme of the lecture is that these sisters should stop being too choosy about their customers; soon enough will come the day when they find the customers too choosy about them.

La Belle Heaulmière was a little too successful for her own good. When she was given chambers in the cloister of Notre Dame Cathedral by Chaplain Nicolas d'Orgemont, the proper ladies of Paris were outraged. They succeeded in sending Chaplain Nicolas to jail and la Belle Heaulmière back to the streets. Long jealous of the handsome appearance of the prostitutes in their finery, the ladies of Paris finally forced the police commander to confine the "daughters of joy" to one neighborhood of the city and to insist that they dress less regally. Their jeweled belts were appropriated for the king's treasury.

A somewhat wry ballade, which Villon scribbled at about the time of this incident, is entitled *Good Advice to Those of Evil Life*. He warns young men not to be trapped into wasting all their money on tarts and taverns, a warning which he rhymed better than he followed. Running down an extensive list of ways to make or lose money which were either illegal or frowned upon, he came to:

> Car or' soyes porteur de bulles,
> Pipeur ou hazardeur de dez,
> Tailleur de faulx coings, tu te brusles,
> Comme ceux qui sont eschaudez,
> Traistres pervers, de foy vuydez,
> Soyes larron, ravis ou pilles:
> Où en va l'acquest, que cuydez?
> Tout aux tavernes et aux filles.
>
> Ryme, raille, cymballe, luttes,
> Comme folz faintis, eshontez;
> Farce, broille, joue de flustes;
> Fais és villes et és citez,
> Fainctes, jeux et moralitez;
> Gaigne au berlan, au glic, aux quilles:
> Où s'en va tout? Or escoutez:
> Tout aux tavernes et aux filles.

> *Envoi*
> Chausses, pourpoinctz, esguilletez,
> Robes, et toutes vos drapilles,
> Ains que soient usez, vous portez
> Tout aux tavernes et aux filles.

If documents you falsify,
Or make fake coins, for which you may—
Beware—be boiled in oil and burning, die—
Or load the dice before you play;
Or if through life you rob your way,
Or in most faithless of the arts—
Treason, excel: where flies your pay?
All to taverns and saucy tarts.

Cheaters at cards and ninepins, too,
Hucksters of fraud, who day to day
Shamelessly swindle, slipping through
City and village and then away;
Musicians, actors, jesters gay,
Who masquerade in buffoon's parts,
Where do our purses ever stray?
All to taverns and saucy tarts.

Envoi

The doublet that bright chevrons splay,
The cloak that over new tights parts,
Go, e'er a wanton reads this lay,
All to taverns and saucy tarts.

But if Villon, like so many of his contemporaries, spent more than he ought on "taverns and tarts"; if he, like others, supported his wastrel tastes by loading the dice, or worse, still he was different from others. He had a way of standing off, catching himself in an act, and recording it. Even though, as he once wrote, his "ink froze at the dead season of the year when the wolves have only the wind to live on,'' his inspiration did not falter.

Whence this fluency? The mystery that still shrouds much of Villon's story conceals the complete answer. Who was his father? We are not positive, and perhaps neither was he. What happened to him, finally? We have no idea. But from what his poetry does tell us about the first thirty-two years of his life, we can piece together most of what set him apart. We can see the contrasts in his nature which later caused him to be romanticized as a hapless saint and condemned as a hopeless sinner, when in truth he was neither one. We can watch him mature from François, the rhymester rogue "born near Pontoise," into Villon the poet of compassion for a generation hurtled hither and yon in the harsh winds of change.

It was this latter Villon who, in a prize-winning ballade, grieved: "I, a stranger in my native land, laugh in tears, knowing nothing is certain but uncertainty. And so at dawn I say, 'God give you good evening.' ''

✣ CHAPTER III ✣

The Rhymester Rogue

François des Loges de Montcorbier, better known as François Villon, was born near the Abbey of the Celestins, on the right bank of the river Seine. Within sight of the blunt twin towers of Notre Dame rising from the mid-Seine Ile de la Cité, this abbey sprawled across spacious grounds. It employed servants by the dozen. François' mother was one of them. His father, most authorities believe, came from a farm fief called Les Loges on the estate of Montcorbier, a landholding of the Duke of Bourbon that straddled the southwest border of Burgundy. Villon never saw the man. His mother took care of the boy as best she could until he was five years old. Then she persuaded Guillaume de Villon, chaplain of the Chapel of Saint John in the nearby Church of Saint Benoît-le-bien-Tourné, to adopt her son. Hence the name by which the poet became known to the world. There is speculation that Guillaume was truly his father; generally he is thought to be an uncle.

Chaplain Guillaume was a man of substantial reputation. A property owner, he rented out as taverns several of his houses in the Saint Benoît community. The wine sold in these taverns was purchased from the chaplain; he had vineyards under cultivation just outside the city gates. That he taught law at the university was not held against him; he was a church lawyer and had the best of relationships with the police and the courts. He probably hoped his adopted son would follow his profession, for the education which he himself gave François until the boy entered the university was slanted toward law. To become a lawyer, François would have needed another two years of study after receiving his Master of Arts degree. He did not choose to continue after the Pet-au-Diable fracas.

Villon was extremely fond of his guardian. In his poetry he calls Guillaume *mon plus que père,* my more-than-father. He recollects that the chaplain reared him "more tenderly than a mother minds a child in swaddling clothes" and, what's more, rescued him from many a scrape which he is sure the good clergyman would have preferred to avoid. These lines of affection occur in a mock will in which the poet leaves his library to Guillaume.

Villon wrote two such wills in verse, remembering friend and foe alike with what he considered appropriate mementos. Like the ballade, the mock will was a conventional poetic form of the Middle Ages—the medieval equivalent of the will which today's high-school seniors sometimes leave to underclassmen. The form of Villon's bequest to his uncle was typical. Although it started with affection, it ended with the tongue-in-cheek deviltry which Villon could rarely resist. To the gift of his library he adds a second souvenir, the scandalous tale he wrote about the Pet-au-Diable affair. He tells his uncle that the manuscript is in the keeping of a famous truthteller, Guy Tabary, who will vouch for the story's honesty. More Villon irony. Tabary was one of Villon's more disreputable friends. As he and his uncle both knew, probably the one time in Tabary's life when this swindler told the unvarnished truth was under torture by *treteau*. The torture extracted from him a list of colleagues in a robbery. Villon's name was on the list and Uncle Guillaume had to pay back Villon's share of the loot. So the verses that started out in filial affection end with a sardonic punch. One can almost see the crooked smile on that mouth deformed by a dagger slash as Villon jabbed the punch lines with his ruthless quill.

But though the chaplain's training fell far short of shaping his ward into a respectable lawyer, it did leave indelible imprints on the poetry the boy grew up to write. The most obvious of Guillaume's imprints is the frequency and ease with which Villon scattered Biblical quotations through his verse, often rhyming the Latin in which the Bible then appeared with the French of his own vocabulary. Villon's pessimistic view of society never shook the faith of his childhood years. In an age of much false piety, he had genuine Christian humility. "I am not a judge," he wrote, "nor commissioned either to punish or absolve others, being of all the most imperfect." Only on one occasion, later in his life, did his poetry sizzle with personal hatred. His normal technique was reportorial. "What I have written, is written," he said. He would let the reader be the judge.

Another seed which life at Saint Benoît planted in the heart of the child François flowered in the poetry of the man: love of France. That he did not share his university's sympathy for Burgundian sell-outs was doubtless due to the staunch pro-French feeling that surrounded him at Saint Benoît. There, too, he had been exposed to thorough discussions about his heroine, Joan of Arc.

When Villon was fifteen, the king, upon whose head Joan had set the crown of France, and who had done nothing to save her from the stake, began to fear that history might record he had been crowned by a witch. Witchcraft had been trumped up as the grounds for her burning. Consequently he ordered a post-mortem retrial of Joan. Three church lawyers from Saint Benoît sat on the jury which cleared Joan's name and the king's throne. During the ten years of jury deliberation, the progress of the retrial was a well-worn topic of conversation from cloister to tavern in the Saint Benoît quarter. The church was especially gratified to have three representatives on the tribunal. These appointments were regarded as a slap in the face to Notre Dame, Saint Benoît's ecclesiastical overseer, which had unsuccessfully tried to silence the parish because of its stubborn pro-French stand in the war years.

We can get a fuller picture of young Villon by focusing on this independent-minded community in which he grew up. At the center was the church itself, a large one for a parish in those days, surrounded by its cemetery, charnel house, cloister, tavern, and the several houses owned by the clergy. Villon lived in one of the houses belonging to Guillaume. It was called la Porte Rouge because one entered through a red door from the cloister. The house had two rooms; Villon's was the smaller of the two. From his single window, he had an intimate view of the life of the church community, as well as a broader view of the hustle-bustle of the neighborhood slanting down to the Seine. From time to time an opening between his room and the larger one in the Porte Rouge also framed some interesting goings-on. The room seems to have been used by some of the Saint Benoît chaplains to make love to their mistresses. Villon recalls one such occasion in a ballade beginning:

> Sur mol duvet assis, ung gras chanoine,
> Lez ung brasier, en chambre bien nattée,
> À son costé gisant dame Sydoine,
> Blanche, tendre, pollie et attintée
> Boire ypocras, à jour et à nuyctee,
> Rire, jouer, mignoter et baiser,
> Et nud à nud, pour mieulx des corps ayser,
> Les vy tous deux, par un trou de mortaise
> Lors je congneuz que, pour deuil apaiser,
> Il n'est tresor que de vivre à son aise.

Cozy the room with tapestry,
Cushy the couch where the fat priest lay
Close to his lady, Sidony;
The brazier coals, a bright bouquet,
Flushed her smooth flesh with rosy ray,
And warmed the wine they sipped at play,
Caressing, kissing, night to day,
Body to body given to please.
Spying, I whispered even as they:
No treasure matches a life of ease.

Possibly Villon recollected the scene from his earliest years
at Saint Benoît, for his *envoi* at the ballade's end declares:

Prince, jugez, pour tous nous accorder.
Quant est a moy, mais qu'a nul n'en desplaise,
Petit enfant, j'ay ouy recorder
Qu'il n'est tresor que de vivre à son aise.

Milord, the proof is yours to weigh.
For me, I wish not to displease,
But since a child, I've heard men say
No treasure matches a life of ease.

Villon, being Villon, is not critical of the priest. Only if he
had heard a priest tout the virtues of chastity from the pul-
pit, while practicing something else in his own life, would
Villon's verse have been critical. He berated hypocrites, not
humans.

Villon had, in fact, an easygoing relationship with all the
Saint Benoît clergy except one, a certain dour and dogged
Laurence Poutrel. The rest of the fathers rather relished
having a poet in their midst. They found his verses entertaining, especially those inspired by their long-time feud
with the priesthood of Notre Dame.

Medieval churches as well as medieval nobles had their
fiefs, and Saint Benoît was a fief of Notre Dame. It was
subject to Notre Dame's orders and taxes. Once a year, on
March 21, Saint Benedict's Day, a lordly representation
from Notre Dame's several hundred chaplains, sixteen
canons, and ten curates paid a visit to the eight chaplains of
Saint Benoît. Perhaps half of the 138 servants who attended
to the needs of Notre Dame dignitaries accompanied their
employers. The retinue proceeded up the hill with acolytes
swinging incense ahead of it and a choir, costumed in embroidered silk and pearl-strewn velour, bringing up the rear,
chanting.

To the people of the Saint Benoît neighborhood, this was
a grand holiday. They shut their shops, twined marjoram in
their hair, and poured out into the streets, parading behind
the visitors. As the procession wound into the nave of the
church, the tag-alongs and the Notre Dame servants
dropped off into nearby taverns. Up the nave the officials
proceeded and into the choir stalls. With a great rustle of
their garments, they seated themselves in the stalls on the
left. Facing them in the right-hand stalls sat the eight

chaplains. In the middle, between the two groups, stood the notary of Saint Benoît.

The ceremony began. It was not a church service but a vehement argument, with the notary vainly trying to umpire. The main purpose of Notre Dame's visit was to collect the tribute money due annually from its fief, as well as a share of the wheat and grapes which the clergy grew just outside the city. The amount was not fixed: Notre Dame pressed for as much as it could get, and Saint Benoît gave as little as it could get away with. Frequently the argument was further embittered by differing politics on the war. On one occasion the dispute became so violent that two priests of Notre Dame set upon the Saint Benoît notary, threw him to the floor, and kicked him in the face. Appealing to the archbishop for redress, Saint Benoît demanded and eventually got from Notre Dame damages of six hundred pounds of silver. When the tribute haggling was finished, a group of the visitors made an inspection tour of the church property, poking diligently into every cranny and crevice to assure themselves that their fief was in a state of good repair.

In a society that was one vast marketplace, clergy were among the shrewdest bargainers. Big churches amassed big fortunes. And the thieves who robbed them of it, when they could, felt no sense of sacrilege. The church was simply where the money was. One can imagine that the annual Notre Dame–Saint Benoît confrontations did nothing to sanctify the image of the Church in Villon's mind. The miracle was that it did nothing to undermine his faith in God.

When the Notre Dame procession left, the Saint Benoît chaplains sagged into the Cuiller, the Spoon, as the cloister tavern was called. *That* was over for another year. On such an occasion, they might well have listened with chuckles to Villon's rhymed barbs aimed at the most important of the visiting personages. To a couple of them the poet graciously offered a pair of rent-free houses. Later in the verse it turns out that one house is a pillory, the other a jail.

These Saint Benoît chaplains were, on the whole, well liked by the people among whom they lived. They had the task of administering justice in the quarter and maintained a jail in their crypt and a gallows in their suburban wheat-field, but the jail gave refuge to beggars grateful for the shelter more often than it confined criminals. The gallows was rarely used. In the neighborhood butcher stall, which belonged to the Saint Benoît clergy, they kept their meat prices as moderate as possible. Every autumn they held a gala market in the cloister, where they sold their grapes and grain, along with other produce contributed to them by farmers. They used half the cloister for their own wares; the other half they rented to local merchants for fees that were well below the rates charged in such places as the Cimetière des Innocents. The fathers didn't grow rich from these endeavors, but they made enough to support themselves comfortably in between the purse-denting visits from Notre Dame.

Villon's section of Paris zigzagged down to the Seine in a confusion of narrow streets which had grown up from the footpaths of the previous century. Each was noted for the specialties of its merchants. There was the street of the herb-sellers, the street of the blacksmiths, the street of the barrel-makers, the shoemakers, the crib-makers, the tailors. From Villon's Porte Rouge window he could see past these shops to the watchtowered wall that looped around the quarter and over the wall to the restless life of the river.

The river was the city's main artery for both commercial and private transportation, and traffic on it was always heavy. Skiffs taxied travelers who could afford the fare, slipping between lumbering barges loaded with wine, wood, charcoal, salt, hay, and grain. The barges tied up at the Ile de la Cité, near Notre Dame. The traffic was regulated by guards whose duties also involved warding off thieves, keeping the river clean and tidy and the riverside ditches clear. The guards could fine any barge caught dumping garbage in the water or any citizen caught pasturing his cows in the ditches. The job of guard was considered a plum. It was understood that guards were allowed to help themselves to goods being unloaded from the barges, and they sometimes did so to an extent which made it difficult to distinguish guards from thieves. They were also allowed to fish in parts of the Seine where fishing was forbidden. They were not supposed to steal ducks in the ditches, but they did.

A couple of Villon's good friends, Jehan le Loup (John the Wolf) and Casin Cholet, were river guards. One of Villon's wills offers them each the ample robe of a friar under which to hide their coveys of stolen ducks.

On embankments above the ditches, and on some of the bridges that spanned the river, were the stalls of licensed grocers, vendors of fish, chickens, eggs, sausages, tripe, venison, and a variety of fruits, vegetables, and nuts. From stall to stall the conversational hum of milling shoppers was pierced by the shrill cries of aggressive merchants: *Vous faut-il point d'angelots? A mes belles oranges! A mes beaux épinards! A mes belles amandes nouvelles!* Don't you need some Brie cheese? Look at my beautiful oranges, my beautiful spinach, my beautiful fresh almonds!

One market in particular, at the Place de Grève, where the barges unloaded to wholesale merchants before tying up, offered sensational diversions. This was the square where condemned criminals about to be hung were paraded round and round in wooden carts, a sight which brought customers in the surrounding taverns reeling to the doors. One of these taverns, the Grand Godet, or Big Drinking Horn, Villon's first will consigned to an alcoholic friend, Jacques Raguer, later to become a bishop. Another popular feature of the square was its celebration of religious festivals and pageants, especially the roaring bonfire which, on the eve of the feast of Saint John, June 23, cast a glow like sunrise over the Seine.

Villon's favorite market had a more piquant distinction. It was located on le Petit Pont, the Little Bridge, which connected the Ile de la Cité with the left bank of the river. The fame of the Petit Pont was its fishmongers—all women. To augment the power of their tongues and lungs, they had a habit of thumping their tubs of fish, so that their sales cries and arguments often were accompanied by the sound of drums. It was these fishmongers whom Villon had in mind when, in his ballade to the women of Paris, he offered to stack "two Paris vendors" against all comers from elsewhere. And well he might. A law which prohibited swearing at a customer or striking him with the merchandise was broadly disregarded on the Petit Pont.

There was also a law against selling spoiled meats, but the butchers who owned the slaughter yard on the Seine a little north of the Petit Pont had built persuasive enough connections with the courts to defy this restriction. And so Villon wishes for a butcher friend, Jehan Tronne, that he may find a tender, fresh lamb to slaughter, and also have:

> A whisk to drive away the flies
> From stench of beef nobody buys.

Near the slaughter yard stood a large drinking trough for
horses, which Villon threw into his bequest to his ever
thirsty friend, Raguer, along with the Drinking Horn
Tavern on the Place de Grève.

Raguer was among the regulars at the Pomme de Pin
tavern, along with Villon, Tabary, Cholet, Jehan le Loup,
René de Montigny, and Colin de Cayeux, a locksmith who
was a lockpicker by night. The tavern keeper, Robin Turgis,
was one of their group, but his friendship didn't lower the
price of his food and drink. Most of the Villon clique had
little to spare; they earned bare livings in petty government
jobs, like Cholet's and Jehan's, or as helpers in tradesmen's
shops, or as church clerks. Villon himself was probably a
clerk for a lawyer or financier.

On the fifth of June, 1455, the twenty-four-year-old
Villon had the day off from work, it being a holy day, la
Fête de Dieu. It was the kind of day on which he would
have paid a visit to the Pomme de Pin, but he would have
left by noon, for in the afternoon he was to be in a procession.
Up, down, and around the hillside streets the procession
wound all afternoon long. In early evening, after the march-
ing was over, Villon sat on the low wall outside the church.
The holiday mood still lingered in the neighborhood. A twi-
light breeze fluttered the flags at every window and wafted
the scent of incense with the warm breath of spring. Villon
probably still wore on his head the wreath of white violets

customary for the fete. With him was a Saint Benoît curate named Gilles and a perky young tart named Isabeau, who was known to be the current property of a priest of another parish, Philippe de Sermoise.

On this evening the priest, accompanied by a clerk, sought out Isabeau and Villon. According to testimony later provided by the clerk and by Gilles, the priest approached "with a furious air." The following conversation took place:

SERMOISE: Master François, I've finally found you. Believe me, I'm angry. I'm going to teach you a lesson.
VILLON: What for? How have I harmed you? Why are you so excited?

Villon stood up and with a gesture offered Sermoise his seat on the wall next to Isabeau. Sermoise shook his head, and Villon, shrugging, sat down again. Whereupon Sermoise whipped a dagger from under his robe and slashed Villon in the face, lip to nostril. Isabeau ran off. Villon, drawing his own dagger, stabbed Sermoise in the groin. Then he ran for the cloister, stooping en route to pick up a rock. Sermoise staggered after him. Villon let fly the rock, which hit Sermoise in the head.

At the sound of the commotion, a crowd gathered. The wounded priest was carried inside and later to a hospital, where he died the next day.

On his deathbed, he was questioned by an examiner

from the Châtelet whose job it was to gather evidence in criminal cases. Sermoise exonerated Villon, without going into the reason why, stating merely that Villon's action was "justified by certain causes which prompted it."

Villon, unaware of the exoneration, had made a hasty exit from Paris. Many crimes were taken lightly in those days, but priest killing was not one of them. Even though two witnesses could, if they would, have sworn that his blows were struck in self-defense, Villon had no intention of waiting to see what the court might decide. Immediately after the fight, he went to a barber to have his wound dressed. Minor surgery and the care of superficial wounds were services offered by all barbers of the time. The barber being required to register the names of his patients with the police, Villon gave him the name Michel Mouton, which the barber doubtless inscribed with a wink. Then Villon returned to his Porte Rouge bedroom, where he gathered a few belongings and wrote two requests for mercy and pardon. One he addressed to a court known as the Little Chancellery in Paris, and signed it François de Montcorbier. The other, signed François des Loges, otherwise known as Villon, appealed to the Grand Chancellery, then on circuit with the king. These courts were under royal jurisdiction.

In January 1456, both Montcorbier and Loges received pardons, identically phrased: "Since the suppliant has until this date conducted himself honorably and well, living, without cause for blame or reproach, a good life and sincere, and has never been arrested or convicted of any other crime; Charles, by Grace of God King of France, preferring mercy to the rigors of justice, forgives and pardons the above-described deed and circumstance, and lays aside all penalties, fines, bodily punishment, and civil or criminal processes attached thereto.''

Villon's conduct, especially in his student days, had not been quite so exemplary as the language of the pardons would suggest. This fact, plus the duplication of phrasing in documents that were not forms, has given rise to the conjecture that Villon himself may have been the author of the text. The good Guillaume, with his high connections, could have seen to it that the text was put into the right hands.

The incident was to have a profound effect on the direction of Villon's life. Up to that June day of the Fête de Dieu, François Villon had been more or less just another young Parisian on the loose, with a distinguishing knack for writing amusing verse. When he returned from his flight from justice, he became something else.

Where had he been, meanwhile? Somewhere just south of Paris. There are several theories as to the precise spot; the best-founded and most entertaining of them places him under the wing of the Abbess Huguette du Hamel. This notorious Mother Superior of the Abbey of Port Royal-des-Champs preferred male clothing to her religious habit, swore like a man, drank like a man, but was entirely feminine when it came to her liking for men. She condoned a similar taste among the nuns in her establishment, and even charged their consorts admission. The revenues were sufficient to prevent her ecclesiastical higher-ups from putting a damper on her activities, which included frequent sorties from her abbey. Of noble birth, and with considerable influence at court, she was routinely invited to many festivities and she was not one to refuse an invitation.

On one sortie she took off with Villon to Bourg-la-Reine, a town not far from her abbey. They stayed for a week at an inn run by the local barber, Perrot Girart, who fed them without charge on suckling pigs. In verse written toward the end of 1461, Villon recalls the sojourn, placing it six years earlier, which would have been during the period of his voluntary exile. In gratitude for Girart's hospitality, Villon offers him a gift for his barbershop:

> Deux bassins et ung coquemart,
> Puisqu'à gaigner mect telle peine.
> Des ans y a demy douzaine
> Qu'en son hostel, de cochons gras
> M'apastela, une sepmaine:
> Tesmoing l'abesse de Pourras.*

* Pourras, meaning rotten, was the popular name for the Abbey of Port Royal-des-Champs.

A kettle and twin basin set,
The which to earn would costly be,
Remembering how he welcomed me.
Those piglets fat I'll not forget—
Six years they've lived in memory:
If you don't believe me—ask Huguette!

It's possible that Huguette may have had a hand, along
with Guillaume, in obtaining the pardons that absolved
Villon of any responsibility for Sermoise's death. When,
these papers in his purse and a whistle on his lips, Villon
returned to his friends at the Pomme de Pin, his sharp-
tongued vendors on the Petit Pont, his beloved Paris that
"had the best of it," he got a rude shock. His job was gone,
and so was his girl.

Despite Villon's escapades with the Huguettes and Isa-
beaus of his day, only two girls captured his heart. The first
was Catherine de Vaucelles, whom he had probably known
since childhood since her uncle, a canon of St. Benoît, lived
next door to Guillaume. Villon had a habit of reciting his
verses under her window in the hope of winning her favor.
On his return to Paris in 1456, he resumed this habit—
only to be treated to a *nuit sanglante à bas chevet*. On
Catherine's orders, Noël de Jolys, a young man who had
always been Villon's rival for her affection, set upon him
and, with the help of several others, stripped and beat him,
leaving him where he lay. As Villon recorded the incident
in a ballade dealing with lovers' woes:

De moy, povre, je vueil parler:
J'en fuz batu, comme à ru telles,
Tout nud, ja ne le quiers celer.
Qui me feit mascher ces groiselles,
Fors Katherine de Vauselles?
Noël le tiers ot, qui fut là,
Mitaines à ces nopces telles . . .
Bien heureux est qui rien n'y a!

Though but a humble suitor I,
I, too, a sordid tale can tell:
How, stripped, whipped, till I feared to die,
Pummeled like washing by Noël,
I was left writhing where I fell.
On her who had me thrashed, cry fie—
To hell with love like yours, Vaucelles,
Lucky the lads it passes by.

And, what is worse, Villon laments:

> Quoy que je luy voulsisse dire,
> Elle estoit preste d'escouter,
> Sans m'accorder ne contredire:
> Qui me plus souffroit acouter,
> Joignant des piés m'arieter,
> Et ainsi m'alloit amusant
> Elle me souffroit tout racompter
> Mais si n'estoit qu'en m'abusant.

> Ever she bent a willing ear
> To all I felt impelled to say,

Never a murmur let me hear
That meant a yes or meant a nay,
But let me, kneeling, have my way—
Amused to play a lover's game,
To let me babble till the day
She could abuse me to my shame.

After recovering from the beating, no doubt the poet treated his bruises of body and soul to some of the free-flowing medicine of the Pomme de Pin. Having lost his job, he would have had to scrape for the wherewithal to pay his bill. It might have been at this time that he pulled a wine and water switch on Robin, the proprietor, which his other friends, who were in on this bit of sleight of hand, found uproarious. We don't know the date of the trick, but we do have a record of the mechanics. Villon entered the tavern with two pitchers: one empty, one filled with water. He asked Robin to fill the empty one with wine. Sampling the contents, he declared the wine no good and ostensibly poured it back in the barrel. Actually he emptied the pitcher of water into the barrel and walked out with the wine.

It was here at the Pomme de Pin, in December of 1456, that Villon and nine others, among whom were Guy Tabary, Colin de Cayeux, and a priest identified only as Nicolas, planned the first real criminal act in which Villon was involved. Had he not lost his job as a result of his flight after the death of Sermoise, would he have thrown in his

lot with the flourishing Parisian underworld? Was the
bitterness and despair, later to become dominant in his writing, already budding? These are questions for speculation:
the answers are not to be found in the scant historical records
of Villon's life or even in his poetry, revealing as it is of the
man's nature. Speculate we must, for there is nothing of
what we know in the affection-surrounded years of his rear-
ing at Saint Benoît which would go into the making of a
career thief. And that is the course on which Villon em-
barked when he and Colin de Cayeux and Guy Tabary and
Father Nicolas and the others planned the robbery of the
College of Navarre.

Navarre, a theological seminary, was one of twenty-two
colleges of the Sorbonne University. It was well known to
be the richest of the twenty-two. At ten o'clock at night,
five days before Christmas, the band from the Pomme de
Pin, having completed their plans, set out for this college.
As the group had decided, Villon was left outside the wall to
keep watch. With him the others left their heavy cloaks,
which would have weighed them down as they scaled the
barrier. Once over it, the priest, Nicolas, who knew the
college layout, led the way to the vault. There, in two chests,
one inside the other, both bound with iron strips and pad-
locked, the gold of Navarre was hidden. Colin de Cayeux
set to work. One! two! three! four! He sprang all four padlocks on the outer chest, while colleagues wrestled with the
iron bands. Three more padlocks confronted Colin on the

inner chest. He pried. And pried. And pried. These locks didn't give so easily.

Outside, Villon paced back and forth in the snow. What was keeping them in there? Somewhere a dog yelped. Once. Twice. Would it attract the guard?

After two hours, Colin managed to force the last lock. Two men lifted the lid back on its hinges, gently, to prevent the sound of creaking. Then each thief filled the pouch at his belt with gold pieces. There was more gold than even the priest had thought—the nine of them couldn't carry it all. But they scooped up five hundred of the heavy coins; later they would divide them evenly, among themselves and Villon. Now, hurriedly leaving the building, they made for the wall.

As Tabary, last in line, started to swing himself up, the yelping dog caught up with them. It gripped Tabary by the ankle, pulling him to the ground. Dog and man rolled over and over. The man fumbled for his dagger, found it, plunged it in the dog's neck, and scrambled up the wall, leaving a crimson trail of blood on the sparkling snow.

The bloody snow and the dead dog commanded only passing attention the next morning. No one caught on to anything amiss at Navarre until two months later, when the time came for the periodic check of the college vault by certified examiners. Even then, when the robbery was discovered, a formality prevented notification of the police. One of the examiners had not been present. When he was later recruited and the police were informed, they made only a lackadaisical effort to solve the crime.

A dean of the college decided to play detective himself. That dean was Laurence Poutrel, the one member of the Saint Benoît clergy who had no liking for François Villon. Did Poutrel suspect that Villon had been involved in the Navarre theft? Perhaps. He had some reason, certainly, to believe that Villon's hangout, the Pomme de Pin, was the place to start hunting for clues. He employed a curate from a parish outside Paris to ingratiate himself with the tavern regulars.

The curate pretended that he knew the whereabouts of considerable church treasure, to which he could lead those able to help him break in. Tabary volunteered his aid and, as credentials for the usefulness of his services, babbled about his bravery when attacked by the dog in the Navarre robbery. He said enough to get himself arrested and under *treteau* gave further details of the crime. This was the incident which prompted Villon to call Tabary the "truthteller." As a result of his confession, those of the thieves who could be located were fined fifty gold pieces each, payable in two installments. The fine was intended to replace the stolen loot. Actually, very little of what was collected found its way back to the pilfered casks of Navarre. It never got farther than the pockets of the police.

François Villon was one burglar nowhere to be found. Almost immediately after the robbery he had thought it prudent to leave Paris. Before his departure, he had stood at the desk in his Porte Rouge bedroom and written out 240 lines of verse, *Le Petit Testament,* The Little Will. *Le Petit Testament* was Villon's first experiment with this medieval form. Later he would use it as a means to convey a social philosophy, reinforced with emotion. This initial try had no such depth. It was mainly a tongue-in-cheek affair, glinting with the irony that was the youthful Villon's shield against the harsh realities of his time. He begins:

> L'an quatre cens cinquante et six,
> Je, François Villon, escollier,
> Considerant, de sens rassis,
> Le frain aux dents, franc au collier,
> Qu'on doit ses oeuvres conseiller,
> Comme Vegece le racompte,
> Saige Romain, grant conseiller,
> Ou autrement on se mescompte.
>
> En ce temps que j'ay dit devant,
> Sur le Noël, morte saison,
> Lorsque les loups vivent de vent.
> Et qu'on se tient à sa maison,
> Pour le frimas, prés du tison,
> Me vint le vouloir de briser
> Ma tres-amoureuse prison,
> Qui souloit mon cueur desbriser.

In the year 1456,
I, François Villon, being sane,
A scholar of good will, affix

My name below and do ordain
My friends shall share my every gain.
As wise Vegetius* once said:
Dispose in life of your domain,
Or else regret it when you're dead.

In this dead season of the year
Near Christmas, when outside my door
The howl of wind and wolves I hear
As wolves dine on the wind's cold core;
In bitter frost which men deplore
While huddling at the fireside,
Now would I up and out, explore
Beyond love's prison where I bide.

The reference to love's prison was pure medieval rhetoric, as were several stanzas that followed, bewailing the scorn with which Catherine de Vaucelles had treated the writer. Not for heartsickness over any woman was Villon taking leave of Paris "in bitter frost." He continues more seriously:

Et puisque departir me fault,
Et du retour ne suis certain:
Je ne suis homme sans deffault,
Ne qu'autre d'assier ne d'estain,
Vivre aux humains est incertain,
Et après mort n'y a relaiz.
Je m'en voys en pays loingtain
Si establiz ce present Laiz.

* A Roman writer, *circa* 385.

No second chance tolls in death's knell,
Certain is life's uncertainty:
Who knows is this my last farewell
As to a country far I flee,
Confessing first impurity?
I am as steel alloyed with tin:
Thus faulted, with humility
These final verses I begin.

The humility that was always Villon's comes through in this verse, as does his ever present consciousness of the nearness of death. But the mood is not maintained. From here on in, he rollicks through a list of legatees for each of whom he has devised a wickedly suitable bequest. It is in the *Petit Testament* that we find the bequests of a flywhisk for Villon's butcher friend, the Drinking Horn tavern and the horse trough for his alcoholic friend, the friars' robes for the duck thieves, and the rent-free use of pillory and jail for the Notre Dame clergy. In addition, he leaves the captain of the guard a *heaulme,* a type of helmet so closed in over the face that it was almost impossible for the wearer to see anything. He describes the three richest loan sharks in Paris as poor little children, naked as worms, and in mock pity leaves each of them a few coins. Police, priests, professors, bankers, barbers, grocers, goldsmiths, thieves, tailors, courtiers, tavern keepers, students—the high and the low parade together through Villon's will, each personality pausing for a verse in which Villon singles out the characteristic of the

man that best lends itself to ridicule. The one serious bequest
is addressed to his *plus que père,* Guillaume:

> Premierement, au nom du Pere,
> Du Filz et du Saint-Esperit,
> Et de la glorieuse Mere
> Par qui grace point ne perit,
> Je laisse, de par Dieu, mon bruit
> A maistre Guillaume Villon
> Qui en l'honneur de ce nom bruit
> Mes tentes et mon pavillon.

> By Father, Holy Ghost and Son,
> By Mary and this Trinity
> Through whom immortal life is won,
> I leave, if so God willing be,
> To Master Guillaume, legatee,
> Whatever verse confers in fame,
> And pray my poems and memory
> May glorify his honored name.

Not until some years later, in his second Testament, did
he add his library and the *Roman du Pet-au-Diable* to his
bequest to Guillaume. This early will was probably written
straight through without interruption. It was Villon's habit
to compose in this fashion. The time must have been around
nine in the evening when he finished, for toward the end
he says:

Finalement, en estrivant,
Ce soir, seullet, estant en bonne,
Dictant ces laiz et depscripvant,
Je ouys la cloche de Sorbonne
Qui toujours à neuf heures sonne
Le Salut que l'Ange predit:
Cy suspendis et cy mys bourne
Pour prier comme le cueur dit.

Here, alone, I think, compose,
And then with pen set down my lay.
Good health inspires me, head to toes;
I am content with what I say.
At nine, with darkening of the day,
The bells in Sorbonne towers peal
The angelus that bids us pray,
And as my heart commands, I kneel.

When he rises from his knees, his mood has changed again.
He is at peace, rather than being inspired "head to toes."
The darkness advances rapidly and with it the cold. Finally
he admits:

Puis que mon sens fut à repos,
Et l'entendement demeslé,
Je cuiday finer mon propos.
Mais mon encre estoit gelé,
Et mon cierge estoit souflée:
De feu je n'eusse pu finer.

C'estoit assez tartevelé.
Pourtant il me convint finer.

My thoughts are clear, my mind is still,
But flames upon the hearthside sink;
I cannot finish for the chill—
The cold has frozen fast my ink,
My candle flickers on the brink
Of darkness. So I say good night
And muffle up for sleep. I think
No wiser ending could I write.

The next morning the verses lay neatly stacked on his desk. The room was empty. He was gone.

❧ CHAPTER IV ❧

The Stranger in His Native Land

He headed first for Angers, capital of the Loire River province of Anjou. He had a relative there, on his mother's side, a monk. When Tabary was tortured for information on Navarre, he not only implicated Villon but also stated that Villon hoped to get information from this relative which would help him and his Paris friends to pilfer several religious establishments in Anjou. However, there is no record that Villon was involved in any such pilfering. Instead, he seems to have curried favor at the court of the Duke of Anjou, popularly known as the Good King René, the kingdom of Sicily being part of the duke's inheritance.

This nobleman, who loved fine furnishings and well-designed gardens, turned his ancestral headquarters at Angers into a veritable museum of courtly living. Outwardly formidable, the castle rose abruptly from a promontory high above the rivers Loir, Sarthe, and Mayenne, at their junction point just before they poured into the Loire. Making his way along any of these rivers, Villon could have seen from far off the castle's seventeen towers of silvery shale, flat stone mortared with lime ash to flat stone, and striped at intervals with bands of white limestone. So impregnable was this massive edifice, standing as high as a fifteen-story building, that the narrow path along the cliff outside its walls was called the "Promenade of the End of the World." There was not even need for water in the surrounding moat, the usual last-ditch protection for medieval strongholds. Instead, deer frolicked on the green grass of its bed.

Once Villon crossed this moat and entered the central courtyard, he was in a different world. The courtyard was a great garden. To the right of it was the royal chapel, gleaming with gemlike panes of stained glass. To the left were the royal apartments, with beamed and gilded ceilings and elaborately tiled floors. In the great hall hung the Apocalypse tapestry, a 551-foot-long series of sixteen-foot-high panels illustrating the Biblical Book of Revelation. This tapestry can still be seen at Angers. Against alternating backgrounds of delicate rose and soft sky blue, angels and saints, patriarchs and demons, beasts of the field and birds of the air spell out the vision of the book's author, Saint John the Divine. The faces are highly expressive. God in his cloud is the very image of jovial beneficence.

With the aesthetic tastes which dictated the décor of the castle, King René combined scholarship. He was an accomplished mathematician and well versed in law and geology. He spoke Greek, Latin, Hebrew, and Catalan, a Spanish-

French dialect. He dabbled in poetry. The courtyard gardens and the great hall of his castle were the scenes of many a festival where strolling players and wandering poets competed for his favor. Perhaps it was with strolling players that Villon came to Angers, for he traveled with such a band during part of his exile. Angers was the sort of environment in which Villon's wit would have won a ready welcome. Nevertheless, he didn't stay there long. All through his exile, he wandered restlessly from place to place. By the time the waxy-petaled camellias in King René's courtyard were blooming salmon, pink, and white, Villon was off again, hiking through the misty springtime of the Loire Valley. For a while he carried a peddler's pack of trinkets and ornaments, ivory combs, knives, rings, and spices. He might have had the luck now and then to acquire a mule. Most middle-class travelers rode them. Ordinary folk walked; soldiers rode horseback; noblemen and women were most often conveyed in carriages.

Villon would not have lacked for companionship; the roads were well traveled. He would have met pilgrims on their way to some shrine, singing loudly in the hope that their chants would ward off thieves. Pages, on whose tunics were emblazoned the coats of arms of their lords and masters, hurried with missives to be delivered to other lords. Students, on their way to the University of Orléans or of Poitiers, joshed with merrymakers en route to country fairs.

At night Villon might have shared a room in an inn

with a half dozen of any of these. Only the very rich could afford separate apartments. If Villon's sales had been low and his purse was flat, he could rest his pack and his back in a free hospice for impoverished travelers. If the hospice was full or too far, he would have camped in a field or crept into a stable late at night, or curled up in a church doorway. He was probably not above stealing a chicken and cooking it over an open fire for supper.

Many of the characters he encountered as he wandered were up to no good. They were horse thieves, highwaymen, or worse. It was at this time that Villon joined the brotherhood of the Coquillards—the Cockleshells—an army of the desperately hopeless and hopelessly desperate. They were the flotsam and jetsam of war, soldiers whose regiments had been disbanded or had disintegrated, men whose estates had been destroyed. They were disillusioned sons of nobility. They were men who couldn't find jobs and wouldn't find jobs. There were about a thousand of them, all told: thieves, counterfeiters, smugglers, scalpers, lockpickers, pickpockets, pimps, and cheaters at dice.

They spoke a jargon of their own, the terms of which were partly metaphorical (*une dupe* was someone to be duped in a dice game), partly sarcastic (*un ange,* angel, was a police guard), and partly taken from Latin, Greek, and Provençal, a dialect spoken in the South of France. The jargon permitted the Coquillards to recognize each other, but more importantly it permitted them to discuss their plans without danger of being understood by anybody else. Essentially, the brotherhood was a medieval mafia. Their headquarters was in the Burgundian city of Dijon—the residence of their king—from which their network of crime fanned out over most of northern France. Each district had its own Coquillard chieftain, or *cagou*. One of his duties was the instruction of new members. He belonged to a council of the Coquillards, known as the "Arch Imps," whose job it was to keep up to date on the newest opportunities and most effective methods for cheating the public and then to pass this news along. There was also an executive council which assisted the king, helped collect taxes from members, and administered Coquillard justice.

The rules for members were strict. All Coquillards were sworn to help brothers in trouble and never to inform on them, to obey without question the chieftains of their districts, to give set percentages of their take to the national organization, and not to plan crimes of their own without informing their local headquarters. In return, members were cut in on opportunities they would have found difficult to come by alone. If a member broke a rule, he was tried in a Coquillard court. If found guilty, he was stabbed and his body thrown in a sewer.

Although Villon was not initiated into the Coquillards until his exile, several of his Paris pals had long been members. They included Colin de Cayeux, who did the lock-picking job at the College of Navarre, and René de

Montigny, the childhood friend who grew up to be a first-class pickpocket but was eventually hanged for alms stealing. René's career was a prime example of what Villon was talking about in a two-line commentary on the prevalence of crime in his era:

> Necessity makes men defy the law
> As hunger makes wolves flee the forest.

René's father had a well-paid job as supply officer for the king's pantry. In 1418 the Burgundians, having taken Paris, forced Montigny Senior into exile. When, with a turning tide in the war, he was able to come home, he found all his property confiscated. The king had fled Paris. Shortly thereafter, René's father died. Young René, with no hope of a job, found himself burdened with the support of a mother and two sisters. The Coquillard *cagou* of Paris, who hung about the courtyard of the Châtelet, saw René's plight and had a remedy for it.

Villon himself turned out to be an industrious Coquillard student. So complete was his command of Coquillard jargon that he was able to write seven ballades in it, one of which was dedicated to René and Colin. The ballades were sermonettes instructing his fellow members on necessary precautions in a way worthy of the slickest *cagou*. He called on Coquillards to keep always in mind the nearness of the gallows and the gaping gates of prison. To avoid these dangers he advised his brothers not to gamble with players smarter than they, not to take unnecessary risks, not to linger at the scene of a crime or look back after leaving it, to be on guard against informers, to plan all projects carefully and stick with the plan, to hide out, or at least wear a disguise for a suitable period after pulling off a coup. It may be that these warnings came from hard experience, for the poet's own career as a roving Coquillard ended in disaster.

After leaving the court of King René, Villon spent some time at Blois, upriver from Angers, at the court of Charles, Duke of Orléans. Villon and the duke had much in common. Charles was an intense patriot whose father had been murdered by Burgundians and who had himself been captured by the English at Agincourt, a violent battle of the Hundred Years' War. Charles had been only twenty-four at the time. The next quarter century of his life was spent in an English prison. There he began to write poetry, full of homesickness for France, heartsickness for his young wife at home, and anguish over the endless war.

When, as a result of Joan of Arc's victories, he was released by the English, he returned to his family castle, devoting his full time to the writing of poetry and to encouraging younger poets. He remodeled much of Blois, once a medieval keep as forbidding as the exterior of Angers, converting it into a Renaissance residence, full of light and air.

His own apartments were situated in a long gallery overlooking the central courtyard. His ceiling beams were alter-

nately painted in rust red and cobalt blue, gilded with fleurs-
de-lis and sheaves of wheat. A similar motif was carried out
on his tile floors. Outside he lightened the heavy stone with
brickwork, and in the gardens which overlooked the Loire
he placed whimsical-faced stone animals to serve as benches.
In these surroundings he gathered poets for sessions in which
they analyzed their work and competed in verse-making
contests. Those unable to visit Blois in person often sent
poems. Charles had the best of all these lyrics copied on fine
parchment and bound in a leather-covered loose-leaf volume
along with poetry of his own. The book, to which he was
constantly adding, stood on a low, easy-to-reach shelf in his
high-arched library.

But though the duke and Villon had in common their
love of poetry and country, they had also sharp differences.
Charles' poems, for all the passion that motivated them,
remained ethereal. The raw subjects with which Villon
dealt—prostitution, death at its ugliest, the misery of the
poor, and the greed and hypocrisy of the rich—were unmen-
tionables at Blois. To Charles, poetry was a game of mel-
lifluous words and lulling music. To Villon, it was the sharp
cry of the soul, whether in mockery or in pain. Charles,
nearing seventy when Villon accepted his invitation to visit
his court, was the last great French poet of the dying Middle
Ages. Villon, then twenty-seven, was the first poetic herald
of the French Renaissance.

Perhaps the most famous of Charles' poems is a limpid
rondel, a poem containing only two, sometimes only one,

rhyme throughout. This particular rondel celebrates the return of the sun in springtime. Its opening stanza:

Le temps a laissié son manteau
        De vent, de froidure et de pluye,
Et s'est vestu de brouderie,
De soleil luyant, cler et beau.
        Il n'y a beste ne oyseau
Qu'en son jargon ne chant out crie:
Le temps a laissié son manteau
        De vent, de froidure et de pluye.
Riviere, fontaine et ruisseau
Portent en livrée jolie,
        Gouttes d'argent et d'orfeverie:
Chacun s'abille de nouveau,
Le temps a laissié son manteau.

The weather drops its overcoat
        Of wind and iciness and rain,
And garbs itself in light again,
Embroidered by each sunbeam mote.
        From beast and bird, from every throat
In every tongue comes one refrain:
The weather drops its overcoat
Of wind and iciness and rain.
        Now gold and silver spangles float
Where fountains, rivers, brooks retain
The sparkling light the days regain;
Decked out anew, all creatures note
The weather drops its overcoat.

Whereas Villon's vision of the impact of sunlight and weather was:

> A vous parle, compaings de galles,
> Qui estes de tous bons accords;
> Gardez-vous tous de se mau hasles,
> Qui noircist gens quand ilz son mortz;
> Eschevez-le, c'est ung mal mors;
> Passez-vous au mieulx que pourez,
> Et, pour Dieu, soyez tous recors
> Qu'une fois viendra que mourrez.

> Listen to me, lighthearted ones
> Who only plot to pleasures gain,
> Black will your corpses be from sun's
> Merciless burn. The gallows chain
> Will swing you shelterless in rain,
> In heat or cold. All die one day
> But in God's name your greed restrain
> And do not swing—to rot away.

Imagine the upturned noses at Blois, scenting the stench of death which these lines conjure up! One can see why Villon was not happy there. The fare was too luxurious and the life too artificial for the taste of a poet whose finest inspiration came from misery, experienced or observed. Still, vagabonds did not easily come by such a roost, nor did poor poets often find such uninterrupted opportunity to concentrate on their craft. And the duke kept needling Villon. The master of the court alone appeared to recognize that

Blois had a genius in its midst—even if that genius did deal with distasteful subjects. His Grace's ardent eyes and soft smile were often turned on Villon. "You can do better than that," he would comment when Villon tossed off a careless set of rhymes. "You have not yet given me poetry worthy of inscribing in my collection."

Villon became determined to be represented in that book. Doubtless he felt he owed recompense to this white-haired, fragile figure who perpetually wore a fur-trimmed velvet cape around his shoulders as if still trying to shake the chill of a quarter century in an English prison. Besides, there was his own pride to satisfy. One can picture Villon escaping the others by wandering out of the castle into the gardens along the bluff above the Loire. Sitting on the back of one of Charles' stone animals, he would have gazed down at a very different river from his fast-swirling, muddy Seine. Lazy, translucent, the Loire took its time, building up sand bars as it sought the sea. "A stranger in my native land." Perhaps it was here that this phrase came to him. Around it he built his entry in the duke's contest for a ballade on the subject "I die of thirst at the fountain's edge."

> Je meurs de seuf aupres de la fontaine.
> Chaud comme feu, et tremble dent a dent;
> Et mon pay suis en terre lointaine;
> Lez un brasier frissonne tout ardent;
> Nu comme un ver, vêtu en president,

Je ris en pleurs et attends sans espoir;
Confort reprends en triste désespoir;
Je m'éjouis et n'ai plaisir aucun;
Puissant je suis sans force et sans povoir,
Bien recueilli, debouté de chacun.

Rien ne m'est sur que la chose incertaine;
Obscur, fors ce qui est tout evident;
Doute ne fais, fors en chose certaine;
Science tiens a soudain accident;
Je gagne tout et demeure perdant;
Au point de jour dis: "Dieu vous donne bon soir!"
Gisant envers, j'ai grand paour de choir;
J'ai bien de quoi et si n'en ai pas un;
Echoite attends et d'homme ne suis hoir,
Bien recueilli, debouté de chacun.

De rien n'ai soin, si mets toute ma peine
D'acquerir biens et n'y suis pretendant;
Qui mieux me dit, c'est cil qui plus m'ataine,
Et qui plus vrai, lors plus me va bourdant,
Mon ami est qui me fait entendant
D'ung cygne blanc que c'est un corbeau noir;
Et qui me nuit, crois qu'il m'aide a povoir;
Bourde, verté, au jour d'hui m'est tout un;
Je retiens tout, rien ne sait concevoir,
Bien recueilli, debouté de chacun.

Envoi

Prince clement, or vous plaise savoir
Que j'entends mout et n'ai sens ne savoir:
Partial suis, a toutes lois commun,

Que fais je plus? Quoy? Les gages ravoir,
Bien recueilli, debouté de chacun.

A stranger in my native land,
I die of thirst where fountains spill,
Sweat with the cold of firebrand
And shiver, fevered with a chill.
In weakness strong, robust when ill,
Naked as a worm, robed like a king,
I laugh in tears, in sobbing sing,
Hope without hope, joy in despair,
Rejoice in cheerless wandering,
Repulsed and welcomed everywhere.

My doubts alone for certain stand;
From certainty my doubts distill;
Happenstance alone is planned;
Luck is half of science' skill.
Inheritor of no man's will,
I wait for legacies to bring
The riches that lose everything.
At dawn, "Good evening" is my prayer
And flat, I falter, stumbling,
Repulsed and welcomed everywhere.

All I own is this empty hand;
With goods not mine my pouches fill.
Who hurts me most, gives me remand;
My dearest friend is he who will
Confuse white swan's with black crow's quill.
Truth echoes with a liar's ring—

For truth and lies are all one thing.
So I, when wise, am unaware,
Most harmed when helped, my traveling,
Repulsed and welcomed everywhere.

Envoi

Milord, regard this offering,
Which little says—and everything.
To all I bow, yet no views share,
Who aim to win your reckoning,
Repulsed and welcomed everywhere.

It sounded like a pleasant piece of banter, this ballade. It did indeed win his Grace's reckoning, the prize in the contest—as well as applause from the other poets. But, as Villon knew, and possibly Charles guessed, the banter was a disguise. Batting truth back and forth like a shuttlecock from opposite ends of a court, Villon hid in airy nothings a confession of his own weaknesses and his reaction to life at Blois. His flesh was living in warm luxury, clothed by his Grace's tailor, well wined, well cared for, but none of these things was his own. That which belonged to him, his naked spirit, shivered and thirsted. His laughter rang hollow; his truest songs were sobs. He recoiled from the welcome given him; he was better off as a vagabond.

So much for Blois. He goes on to self-analysis. Certain of nothing in his life, he fritters it away, longing for the very comfort he despises when he gets it, longing for the ease which kills his creativity. He has earned nothing. Let's face it—he is even a thief, and his worst enemies are those who get him out of the scrapes he gets himself into. What's more, he is a bit of a liar, bowing to opinions he doesn't share. But what the devil, some of his best friends are liars too, and the distinction between truth and lies is, after all, slight. Look how he has hidden the truth under lies in this poem, in an endeavor to win the prize. The only real truth, real wisdom is instinctive. All else is artificial.

As soon as Villon had won the prize, he left Blois. Apparently he continued downriver to Orléans, where he got into some kind of maladventure, for he was thrown into jail there. He was released when the birth of a daughter to Charles was celebrated by the freeing of prisoners in all the jails of his domain. In gratitude for his liberty, Villon addressed a group of three poems to the infant. A year later he was again in trouble, this time for his role in what was probably a Coquillard project, the theft of a silver chalice from a church.

The church was in the territory of the Archbishop of Orléans, Thibaud d'Aussigny. A wily politician, this archbishop had wangled his appointment through well-placed connections—despite opposition from the king and the Pope. D'Aussigny was a good administrator who founded monasteries, built churches, and saw to it that they were kept in repair. But he was thoroughly hated. He laid down laws that priests and monks were not to wear jewels and fancy shoes and not to surfeit themselves with fine food. When his dictum on dining had little effect, he went further and prescribed exact menus and precise mealtimes. He cut the pay of any priest who did not conform. At this point, the priests in his territory got together and burned out his vineyards. When he replanted them, he took the reluctant precaution of restoring the pay cuts.

Very much of a law-and-order man, the archbishop administered a justice keynoted by severity. Forgiveness of sins was not in his book. When Villon was apprehended after the theft of the chalice, d'Aussigny had him tortured and then thrown into the deepest dungeon of the tower of Manasses, a medieval keep in the Loire Valley town of Meung, between Blois and Orléans.

It was a dread prison and a dreadful cell, infested with vermin, overrun by rats. Through a trap door in the ceiling, bread and water were lowered to the prisoner at intervals. He saw light only when this door was lifted. The cell was below ground level, its exterior walls washed by the Loire, so that inside they dripped with constant damp. Villon became ill, probably of tuberculosis, for he later speaks of "spitting white and thick as cotton," and possibly also of rheumatism.

In the Tour de Manasses he was confined for a year. He described his condition in a letter to his friends, written in ballade form, which, appealing for their help, contrasted his life with theirs. Somehow, he must have persuaded one of

the prison guards to give him paper, pen, and ink, let a shaft
of light through the trap door, and then smuggle the letter
out. It read:

Ayez pitié, ayez pitié de moy,
A tout le moins, si vous plaist, mes amis!
En fosse giz, non pas soubz houx ne may,
En cest exil ouquel je suis transmis
Par fortune, comme Dieu l'a permis.
Filles, amans, jeunes, vieulx et nouveaulx,
Danceurs, saulteurs, faisans les piez de veaux,
Vif comme dars, agus comme aguillon;
Gousiers tintans, clers comme gastaveaux,
Le lesserez là, le povre Villon?

Chantres, chantans à plaisance, sans loy;
Galans, rians, plaisans en faictz et diz;
Coureux, allans, francs de faulx or, d'aloy;
Gens d'esperit ung petit estourdiz:
Trop demourez, car il meurt entandiz.
Faiseurs de laiz, de motets et rondeaux,
Quand mort sera, vous luy ferez chandeaux.
Il n'entre, où gist, n'escler ne tourbillon;
De murs espois on luy a fait bandeaux:
Le lesserez là, le povre Villon?

Venez le veoir en ce piteux arroy,
Nobles hommes, francs de quars et de dix,
Qui ne tenez d'empereur ne de roy;
Mais seulement de Dieu de Paradiz:

Jeuner luy fault dimanches et mardiz,
Dont les dens a plus longues que ratteaux;
Après pain sec, non pas après gasteaux
Bas enterré, table n'a ne tretteaux;
Le lesserez là, le povre Villon?

Envoi

Princes nommez, anciens, jouvenceaux,
Impetrez-moy graces et royaulx sceaux,
Et me montez en quelque corbillon.
Ainsi le font l'un à l'autre pourceaux,
Car, où l'un brait, ilz fuyent à monceaux.
Le lesserez là, le povre Villon?

My friends, I beg you now, I pray
For pity's sake to pity me;
Far from the festival of May
I lie in jail by fate's decree,
Nor dance beneath the holly tree.
Lads and lovers, groom and bride,
Pirouetting side by side
While bells make music in the air:
Remember as you nimbly glide
The poor Villon, will you leave him there?

Singers spontaneous and gay,
Sweethearts laughing with joy and glee,
Moneyless madcaps on your way
To nowhere, jesting merrily:
Villon dies while you caper free.
Poets, musicians, will you provide

Him candles only when he's died?
He suffocates in darkness where
The walls press in on every side:
The poor Villon, will you leave him there?

Come see for yourself his disarray,
Ye men of noble pedigree
Who need no kingdom's taxes pay,
To God alone bending your knee
And scorning other fealty:
Flat on the ground must he abide;
No bench nor bed is at his side,
Stale bread is all his daily fare.
With teeth like rake's and bowels untied,
The poor Villon, will you leave him there?

Envoi

Milords whoever qualified
To have my sentence modified,
I beg you raise me from this lair.
Even the pigs have too much pride
To let such fate a pig betide:
The poor Villon, will you leave him there?

The appeal produced no results. But in October of 1461, Louis XI, about to become King of France, passed through Meung on his way to his coronation in Paris. All prisoners were freed in Louis' honor, Villon included. Among the first verses he set down after his release from the archbishop's prison were:

Et s'aucun me vouloit reprendre
Et dire que je el mauldys,
Non fais, si bien le sçait comprendre,
Et rien de luy je ne mesdys.
Voycy tout le mal que j'en dys:
S'il m'a esté misericors,
Jesus, le roy de paradis,
Tel luy soit à l'ame et au corps!

S'il m'a esté dur et cruel
Trop plus que je ne le racompte.
Je vueil que le Dieu éternel
Luy soit doncq semblable à ce compte!
Mais l'Eglise nous dit et conte
Que prions pour nos ennemis.
Je vous dirai: J'ay tort et honte
Quoy qu'il m'ait faict, à Dieu remis!

Let no man say that I do wrong
Or speak of Thibaud calumny;
Himself he knows no words are strong
Enough to thank him suitably
For mercy that he showed to me.
So here is all I have to say:
Jesus in heaven grant that he
Find mercy in the same degree!

If greater was his cruelty
Than I do in this verse reveal,
May God eternal faithfully
Reward him and with Thibaud deal

As Thibaud dealt with me, so seal
The account. For enemies we must,
The Church insists, to God appeal.
Gladly I do. In God I trust!

He goes on to invoke in Thibaud's behalf verse 7 of Psalm 109, which reads: "Let his days be few and let another take his office!" Thibaud d'Aussigny was the only man of whom Villon wrote with such vitriol. He was angered and hurt by Catherine de Vaucelles; he ridiculed and exposed the hypocrites of Notre Dame; he resented the injustices of his society; but his feelings for Thibaud went far beyond any of these. With all his heart he loathed him. Thibaud had taken a year out of his life, and would have taken more if it hadn't been for "the good King Louis of France," to whom Villon prays that "God will give the honor and glory of Solomon."

He was free, now; once more in light and air. His thoughts turned to Paris. Surely the Navarre affair had by this time been forgotten. It would be safe to go home. But first he needed money. Paris was no city for a man who was broke. He well remembered his penniless return after being absolved of responsibility for the death of the priest Sermoise. *That* had led him to Navarre. Significantly, he did not rob for what he needed now. The Meung dungeon had sobered Villon in many respects which would later give new depth to his poetry. The immediate effect was to restrain him, at least for the present, from tangling with the law.

Instead, he decided to ask for a loan from the Duke of Bourbon, liege lord of the territory from which Villon's father had supposedly come. The duke had loaned Villon a small sum prior to the Meung imprisonment. Tactfully Villon addressed to him a ballade apologizing for not having yet repaid the earlier loan, but guaranteeing that he would repay it, as well as the new one, in very short order. It was a touchy request, begging money from one to whom he was already in debt, and he thought it best to deliver the ballade in person. He started hiking south to Moulins, the duke's capital.

The lack of direct roads necessitated a zigzag route. First he traveled southwest in Poitou, following the reedy banks of the wide river Vienne as it wound around occasional red-roofed villages. In one of these villages he met two young girls who he says were very kind to him, took him in, and taught him to speak the Poitevin dialect of the region. He refuses to repeat their names or addresses, for fear others will take advantage of them.

It is probable that he paused for another brief rest in the clifftop Poitevin capital of Poitiers, where he would have found compatible company among the university students. When the newly cast bell in the old square-towered Church of Saint Porchaire called his companions to classes, he might have visited the nearby house where his heroine, Joan of Arc, had been questioned by scholars and theologians before being allowed to take command of the royal army. Or perhaps he offered a prayer in the tiny church on the market-place, called, ironically, Notre Dame the Big. Its three towers, in the image of pine cones, were roofed by over-lapping hexagonal tiles, their slate quarried from the hills of Poitou.

Did these Pomme de Pin towers, as they were called, bring back to mind his Parisian hangout of the same name? He doesn't say so in his poetry, but it seems likely.

Diarylike as much of Villon's poetry is, it tells us very little about his exile, except to list the places he went, some of his occupations en route, and to describe his anguish in Meung. The truth probably is that he wrote very little during this period. The only poems that have survived are the letter to his friends from Meung, his acknowledgment to Duke Charles' infant daughter for his release from jail in Orléans, his appeal for funds to the Duke de Bourbon, and his prize-winning ballade at Blois. We know from references in records of court life at Blois that he wrote some other verses while there, but they have vanished. The sarcastic lines he let fly at Thibaud d'Aussigny were not set down until he returned to Paris.

Two of the poems from his exile are strictly business, a thank-you letter and a begging letter. The other two throb with homesickness. All France lay before him: its coastal cities in whose harbors rocked the purple-sailed vessels of

Arab traders from North Africa; its villages in whose squares, flag-hung on festive days, wandering poets and storytellers held crowds spellbound, its crisscross of rivers sometimes gnawing crookedly through deep gorges and frothing over boulders, in other places broadening into tranquil lakes. His could be the perfume of wild thyme and of lavender clumps, the clean country scent of poppy-strewn wheatfields, where the ripening grain billowed golden in the breeze. He could draw lungsful of clear air as he climbed snow-glistened mountain slopes. The softness of pine needles could cushion his feet or the black shade of cypresses shelter him in the heat of the day.

No. He wanted only Paris.

You could have the fresh air, the fields and the mountains. Give him the perfume of rotting meat in the Paris butcher stalls. You could take your rivers and lakes; give him the ditches of the Seine. A fiddle-faddle for pine needles. He preferred the cobbles that paved the way up Mont Sainte Geneviève. Give him the Saint John's bonfire in the Place de Grève rather than pages lighting the wall torches in the tapestried great hall of Angers. Give him Saint Benoît's stone wall on a pleasant evening and let Charles d'Orléans keep his stone animal benches in the garden above the Loire.

Villon's Paris had the best of it.

And to regain it, he was forced to travel away from it! Paris lay to the north; money to get there was in the south.

Impatient, he must have often attempted to short-cut through field and forest, for he later recalls that, from Paris to the farthest point his readers may be pleased to imagine, there is neither

> Briar, bramble, nor prickly thorn
> By which Villon was left untorn.

So at last he reached Moulins. He gives us no details of his stay there, saying only that it was a "good town," and that he received the money for which he asked. He made the 450-mile trip from Meung through Poitou to Moulins and back north to Paris in two months. His stopovers in places like Poitou could not have been frequent or long, considering that most of this distance was probably covered on foot. Already ill when he was released from prison, by the time he reached Paris he was not only ill but exhausted. He had to go to bed, too weak even to clutch a quill.

Having written so little in so long, now that he was back in Paris he *wanted* to write! He *would* write. He hired a clerk, Fremin, to take down the poetry he dictated.* Fremin was a little deaf, and inclined to nod off in the middle of one

---

* There has been doubt in some scholars' minds as to whether Fremin was a real person or a figment of Villon's imagination. I do not share this doubt. Villon's poetry was much too factual for such license. All his other characters are real; why invent Fremin?

of Villon's lines—not the greatest recommendation for a clerk. As Villon describes these handicaps:

> Enregistrer j'ay faict ces ditz
> Par mon clerc Fremin l'estourdys,
> Aussi rassis que je puys estre . . .
> S'il me desment, je le mauldys:
> Selon le clerc est deu le maistre.
>
> Somme, plus ne diray qu'ung mot,
> Car commencer vueil à tester:
> Devant mon clerc Fremin qui m'ot
> (S'il ne dort), je vueil protester
> Que n'entends homme detester.
>
> My clerk—Fremin the deaf's his name—
> Takes down my words—I hope the same
> As those I have most carefully
> Designed. For if he errs, the blame
> Will be transferred from him to me.
>
> As I commence to testify
> I swear that from no man I keep
> His just deserts—and none pass by.
> My clerk will witness: all men reap
> Their dues—unless he is asleep.

For six months Villon holed up with Fremin in a rented room, composing steadily. Why did he choose to rent a room instead of returning to Saint Benoît and the haunts of which he had dreamed? It may be that the *Grand Testament,* The Great Will, which he wrote at this time was more than a form. He may have believed that he actually was dying, for he observes, "My heart is growing weak and I feel the thirst of death." Under these circumstances, he could well have felt the need to concentrate on his writing in solitude, fearing little time was left to him and that the temptations of his old neighborhood would shorten even that. Or perhaps he was afraid to face the kindly *plus que père* that his career had done nothing to reward. Possibly both reasons combined to keep him in a remote section of the city.

Whatever the case, we can be grateful, for it was during this period, from December 1461 to the early summer of 1462, that he wrote the greater part of his most profound poetry. In the almost fifteen hundred lines of the *Grand Testament* and in the sixteen ballades and three rondeaux with which he strewed it, he became the master of his talent. Flat on his back in that rented room with his sleepy old deaf clerk, the mature Villon was born.

CHAPTER V

The Poet of
Conscience and Compassion

In his subterranean prison cell in Meung, Villon had had
more than enough time for reflection. And for regrets. In
his rented room in Paris, the regrets poured out into the
beginning of the *Grand Testament,* a long sigh in rhyme.

> Ho, Dieu! se j'eusse estudié
> Au temps de ma jeunesse folle
> Et à bonnes meurs dedié,
> J'eusse maison et couche molle!
> Mais quoy? Je fuyoye l'Escolle,
> Comme faict le mauvays enfant . . .
> En escrivant ceste parolle,
> A peu que le cueur ne me fend.
>
> Mes jours s'en sont allez errant,
> Comme, dit Job, d'une touaille
> Sont les filetz, quand tisserant
> Tient en son poing ardente paille:

Lors s'il y a nul bout qui saille,
Soudainement il le ravit.
Si ne crains plus que rien m'assaille,
Car à la mort tout s'assouvit.

If only, God, when I was young
And thoughtless, had I thought at all—
If youthful vim I had not flung
To winds of whim I might now call
Some house my home, and weary, fall
On softest couch and rest. Alack,
The child who quit school now drinks gall,
Heartsick for time he can't bring back.

All my days have disappeared
Much, as Job said, the raveled ends
Of toweling are neatly sheared
Or burned away as flame ascends
From weaver's torch till there extends
No shred of thread. So I, bereft
Of tiniest time to make amends,
Must face that only death is left.

In this mood, he examined himself, asking the question every close reader of Villon has asked ever since: why did he choose a rogue's career? His own answers, produced in a ballade which he called *Debate between the Heart and Body of Villon,* are no more satisfactory than anyone else's. Here are some of the excuses from that ballade:

Qu'est-ce que j'oy?·

        —Ce suis je.·

           —Qui?

              —Ton cueur.

Qui ne tient qu'à ung petit filet.
Force n'ay plus, substance ne liqueur,
Quand je te voy retraict ainsi seulet,
Com povre chien tappy en recullet.
—Pourquoy est-ce?

        —Pour ta folle plaisance.
—Que t'en chault-il?·

        —J'en ay la desplaisance.
—Laisse m'en paix!

        —Pourquoy?

          —J'y penseray.
—Quand sera-ce?·

      —Quand seray hors d'enfance.
—Plus ne t'en dy.

      —Et je m'en passeray.

J'en ay le dueil; toi le mal et douleur.
Si fusse ung povre ydiot et folet,
Au cueur eusses de t'excuser couleur:
Se n'as-tu soing, tout ung tel, bel ou laid,
Ou la teste es plus dure qu'ung jalet,
Ou mieulx te plaist qu'honneur ceste meschance.
Que répondras à ceste consequence?
—J'en seray hors, quand je trespasseray.
—Dieu! quel confort!

      —Quelle saige eloquence!

—Plus ne t'en dy.
                  —Et je m'en passeray.
D'ond vient ce mal?
                 —Il vient de mon malheur.
Quand Saturne me feit mon fardelet,
Ces maulx y mist, je le croy.
                    —C'est foleur:
Son seigneur es, et te tiens son valet.
Voy que Salomon escript en son roulet:
"Homme sage, ce-dit-il, a puissance
Sur les planetes et sur leur influence."
—Je n'en croy rien: tel qu'ils m'ont faict seray.
—Que dis-tu?
           —Rien.
                —Certes, c'est ma créance.
—Plus ne t'en dy.
                 —Et je m'en passeray.

What do I hear?
            —It is I, your heart.
                 —Who?
—Your heart that clings, though by a slender thread,
To life, which languishes at sight of you
Recoiling like a frightened quadruped,
Whining, deserted in your lonely bed.
—Why am I so?
              —Your sins have brought you there.
—What's that to you?
             —The consequence I bear.

—Leave me in peace.
　　　　　　—Why?
　　　　　　　　　　　—That I may shed
My vices.
　　　　—When?
　　　　　　　　　—With age comes greater care.
—I'll say no more.
　　　　　　　　—Nor I, more than I've said.

Look how I mourn your pain, so plain to view.
If you were but a fool, of half-wits bred,
Excuses could I make and pity you;
But offered good, you choose the bad instead:
It seems to me you are a shingle-head
To take delight in shunning all that's fair:
Or else, perhaps, you simply do not care.
What do you say?
　　　　　　　—My heart, when I am dead,
This one poor life will be no man's affair.
—I'll say no more.
　　　　　　　—Nor I, more than I've said.

What makes you as you are?
　　　　　　　　　　—Fate's crew,
The stars. Saturn no doubt deposited
His evil in my pack, to my soul's rue.
—Come, come, leave off this superstitious dread!
Surely Solomon's wisdom you have read
In which the power of man, he did declare,
Ruled stars. No star a man's power can impair.

—I do not believe him. I am limited
By stars' design to what must be, I swear.
—I'll say no more.
                              —Nor I, more than I've said. . . .

Mingled with such regrets for his own shortcomings were
regrets for lost friends. His return to Paris in 1461 was not
the happy homecoming he had anticipated. Time and death
had taken their toll. Two of his closest companions, the
Coquillards Colin de Cayeux, who had picked the Navarre
locks, and pickpocket René de Montigny, with whom he
had grown up, had been hanged. Tabary had disappeared.

Catherine de Vaucelles he had long since given up hope
of winning. But even the girl who had, at least to some
extent, replaced Catherine in his affections, a girl sometimes
called Marthe, sometimes Rose, would have nothing more
to do with him. A third young woman, whom he does not
name but with whom he seems to have had a happy relationship, had died in his absence.

For these girls, and for Colin and René, he wrote dirges.
The verses for the latter pair pointed to their hanging as a
warning to other Coquillards. Villon wrote the verses in the
Coquillard jargon, addressing them particularly to some of
the brothers taking their ease in Ruel, a town outside Paris,
after having pulled off a *piperie,* jargon for a theft. Villon
seems to have gotten word, or had some hunch, that they too
were in danger.

Coquillars, arvans a Ruel
Menys vous chante que gardez
Que n'y laissez corps et pel,
Comme fist Colin l'Escailler.
Devant la roe a babiller
Il babigna pour son salut!
Pas ne sçavoil oignons peler,
Dont l'amboureux luy rompt le suc.

Changez vos andosses souvent
Et tirez vous tout de droit au temple;
Et eschequez tost, en brouant,
Qu'en la farte ne soiez emple;
Montigny y fut par exemple,
Bien attaché au halle grup
Et y jargonnast il le tremple—
Dont l'amboureux luy rompt le suc.

Coquillards lazing in Ruel,
I warn you: watch, lest you too swing,
Losing body and breath as well,
Like Colin, once of locks the king,
Who under torture loud did sing.
How naïve could Colin be
To hope that this would freedom bring!
The hangman broke his neck with glee.

Your way of dressing change you must;
Disguise yourselves from hat to shoe
And fly Ruel, nor even trust
Flight or disguise, but hide from view.

Lest, like Montigny, also you
Will dance involuntarily.
In jargon, choked, his last breath flew—
The hangman broke his neck with glee.

The poem for Marthe,* although a plea for pity, is in
some ways no gentler than his stark description of Colin's
and René's last moments. The verses are notable not only
for a touch of longing but for a trick which Villon employed
in several other poems, making the first letters of lines spell
out names, his own or others'. In this *Ballade to His Beloved,* the first letters of lines in the first stanza spell Françoys,** and in the second stanza, Marthe.

*F*aulse beaulté, qui tant me couste cher,
*R*ude en effet, hypocrite doucleur,
*A*mour dure plus que fer à mascher:
*N*ommer te puis, de ma deffaçon soeur,
*C*herme felon, la mort d'ung povre cueur,
*O*rgeuil mussé, qui gens mets au mourir,
*Y*eulx sans pitié! Ne veult droict de rigueur,
*S*ans empirer, ung povre secourir?

*M*ieulx m'eust valu avoir esté crier
*A*illeurs secours, c'eust esté mon bonheur:

* Some scholars maintain that this ballade was written at the
court of Charles d'Orléans and inserted by Villon in his Testament.
They believe Marthe to have been a lady at Charles' court. Others,
of whom I am one, believe there is insufficient evidence to warrant
this conclusion.
** Françoys is the medieval French spelling of François.

Rien ne m'eust sceu de ce fait arracher.
Trotter m'en fault en fuyte à deshonneur.
Haro, haro, le grant et le mineur!
Et qu'est cecy? Mourray sans coup ferir,
Où pitié peult, selon ceste teneur,
Sans empirer, ung povre secourir.

Un temps viendra, qui fera desseicher,
Jaulnir, flestrir, vostre espanie fleur:
J'en risse lors, s'enfant peusse marcher
Mais las! nenny. Ce seroit donc foleur.
Vieil je seray; vous laide et sans couleur.
Or, beuvez fort, tant que ru peult courrir,
Ne donnez pas à tous ceste douleur,
Sans empirer, ung povre secourir.

Envoi

Prince amoureux, des amans le greigneur,
Vostre mal gré ne vouldroye encourir,
Mais tout franc cueur doit, par Nostre Seigneur,
Sans empirer, ung povre secourir.

False beauty who has cost me dear,
Rude in truth, falsely discreet,
And love that is for steel veneer,
Name that can to my sure defeat
Charm my heart to its final beat,
Oh, pride that joys to hear men sigh,
In you shall I no pity meet?
Succor me, love, before I die.

More likely loves that hover near
Already love with love to greet,

Regard my plight and offer cheer,
These beckon me to make retreat.
Help, help, untie my tethered feet
Entangled so they cannot fly,
Or else take pity on me, sweet,
Succor me, love, before I die.

Time will fade, turn yellow and sere
Your flowerlike features. Time is fleet
And beauty, too. Then shall I jeer
If still my jawbone is complete.
But no, for age to me will mete
The same sad fate. Ere life wings by,
Drink deep—nor fear to be replete;
Succor me, love, before I die.

Envoi
Milord of love whom these words greet,
Spurn not, I beg, this true heart's cry:
With God upon his mercy seat,
Succor me, love, before I die.

From this plea to a living love, Villon went on to mourn
for a dead one. To the nameless girl who had died, he dedicated a fragile rondel whose charm conjures up the image
of a willow-the-wisp maiden:

Mort, j'appelle de ta rigueur,
Qui as ma maistresse ravie,
Et n'es pas encore assouvie
Se tu ne me tiens en langueur.

Onc puis n'euz force ne vigueur!
Mais que te nuy soit-elle en vie,
    Mort?

Deux estions, et n'avions qu'un cueur!
S'il est mort, force est que devie,
Voire, ou que je vive sans vie
Comme les images, par cueur,
    Mort!

Death, from your harshness I appeal,
Who has my mistress raped from me,
Nor will give over enmity
Till her death with my own you seal.
My worthless life lacks strength and zeal,
But in her life, what injury,
    Death?

Two were we who as one did feel,
She being dead, dead must I be,
Or else live on as lifelessly
As dreams remembered but not real,
    Death!

In spite of his protests, Villon, back from exile, seems to have accepted the loss of love from his life with somewhat more resignation than had been his custom. He inserted in the Testament the bitter verses he had earlier written about Catherine de Vaucelles, and their defiant lines contrast sharply with lines addressed to women after his return. In an entirely different key from his "To hell with love like yours, Vaucelles" is this gentle confession of inadequacy, directed to another of his sometime girlfriends:

> Qu'est-ce a dire? Que Jehanneton
> Plus ne me tient pour valeton,
> Mais pour ung viel usé regnart . . .
> De viel porte voix et le ton,
> Et ne suis qu'ung jeune coquart.
>
> Jeanneton, what shall I say?
> There is no use in me today:
> A rooster, ready for the block,
> That cackles all the day away
> Seem I, though really a young cock.

More than ever, he is preoccupied with the brevity of life, the inevitability of death, and now also with the transiency of youth. He feels caught in a trap set by fate. Was this an attempt to excuse himself, to avoid remorse? His reference to Saturn who "deposited his evil in my pack," in the debate between the heart and the body, hints that part of him would like to deny responsibility for his own actions. He lived, after all, in an age of belief that men's fortunes could be controlled by the stars. Even kings were guided by the advice of astrologers, whom they hired in much the same capacity as modern statesmen may hire polltakers. Whether or not Villon believed in fate, he certainly believed in fatality. One of the short, musing poems written in this time of despair conveys his conviction that what must be, must be:

Au retour de dure prison
Ou j'ay laissé presque la vie,
Se Fortune a sur moy envie,
Jugez s'elle fait mesprison!
Il me semble que, par raison,
Elle deust bien estre assouvie,
　　　Au retour.

Cecy plain est de desraison
Que vueille que du tout desvie,
Plaise à Dieu que l'ame ravie
En soit, lassus, en sa maison,
　　　Au retour!

On return from dungeon where
In cruel hands I all but died,
Have I not judgment satisfied,
Or must I further grievance bear?
It seems to me if fate were fair
The doom that dogs me should subside
　　　On return.

But if there waits some deeper snare
To catch my very life beside,
May God lassoo and snatch inside
His house my soul; so goes my prayer
　　　On return!

Although these later verses of Villon echo with a new
tone of personal resignation, the tone does not carry over into
his assessment of the social order. His bitterness against society's disregard for the poor, the driven, and the unfortu-

nate is deeper than ever. Does a beggar stand outside his window or knock at his door? Villon reads his heart and writes:

> Or luy convient-il mendier,
> Car à ce force le contraint.
> Regrette huy sa mort, et hier,
> Tristesse son cueur si estrainct:
> Souvent, se n'estoit Dieu qu'il crainct,
> Il feroit un horrible faict.
> Et advient qu'en ce Dieu enfrainct,
> Et que luy-mesmes se deffaict.

> By hunger forced, he begs his bread—
> Not of his own will his demand;
> He wishes daily he were dead
> And need not hold out pleading hand.
> Did he not fear his God's command
> He would have ended long e'er now
> A life which offers no remand—
> And may well end it, anyhow.

This verse from the *Grand Testament* is typical of Villon's technique in treating social unbalance—not exactly a lyrical topic. The call to social justice, a natural subject for a sermon, a newspaper editorial, or a political campaign speech, does not so easily come off as poetry. What saved Villon's poems of protest from dullness or rant was their humanity. He exposed injustice, not by attacking the unjust, but by sympathizing with their victims. It is the plight of these victims, be they hungry beggars or hanged pickpockets, that strikes the heart, as poetry must do to be poetry.

Perhaps the most trenchant illustration of this gift for interpreting misery is his *Les Regrets de la Belle Heaulmière*. During Villon's five-year exile, that queen of Paris prostitutes had aged into a pathetic caricature of herself. If such a woman had possessed the skill to record her rue, the record might have been noteworthy. But for a *man* to be able to step inside her shoes and understand her feelings required uncommon sensitivity. It took François Villon to be able to write:

> Advis m'est que j'oy regretter
> La belle qui fut Heaulmière,
> Soy jeune fille souhaitter
> En parler en ceste maniere:
> "Ha! viellesse felonne et fiere,
> Pourquoy m'as si tost abatue?
> Qui me tient, que je ne fiere
> Et qu'à ce coup je ne me tue?
>
> "Tollu m'as ma haulte franchise,
> Que beaulté m'avoit ordonné
> Sur clercz, marchans et gens d'Eglise:
> Car alors n'estoit homme né
> Qui tout le sien ne m'eust donné,
> Quoy qu'il en fust des repentailles,
> Mais que luy eusse abandonné
> Ce que reffusent truandailles.

"À maint homme l'ay reffusé
(Qui n'estoit à moy grand saigesse),
Pour l'amour d'ung garson rusé,
A qui je en faisoie largesse.
A qui que je feisse finesse,
Par m'ame, je l'amoye bien!
Or ne me faisoit que rudesse,
Et ne m'amoit que pour le mien.

"Si ne me sceut tant detrayner,
Fouller aux piedz, que ne l'aymasse,
Et m'eust-il faict les rains trayner,
S'il m'eust dict que je le baissasse
Et que tous me maux oubliasse,
Le glouton, de mal entaché
M'embrassoit. . . . J'en suis plus bien grasse!
Que m'en reste-t-il? Honte et peché.

"Or il est mort, passe vingt ans,
Et je remains vielle chenue.
Quand je pense, las! au bon temps,
Quelle fus, quelle devenue,
Quand me regarde toute nue,
Et je me voy si tres changée,
Povre, seiche, maigre, menue,
Je suis presque toute enragée.

"Qu'est devenu ce front poly,
Ces cheveulx blonds, sourcilz voultyz,
Grande entr'oeil et regard joly
Dont prenoye les plus subtilz,

Ce beau nez droit, grant ne petiz,
Ces petites joinctes oreilles,
Menton fourchu, cler vis traictis,
Et ces belles levres vermeilles?

"Ces gentes espaules menues,
Ces bras longs et ces mains traictisses,
Petis tetins, hanches charnues,
Eslevées, propres, faictisses
A tenir amoureuses lysses,
Ces larges reins, ce sadinet,
Assis sur grosses fermes cuysses,
Dedans son joly jardinet?

"Le front ridé, les cheveulx gris,
Les sourcilz cheuz, les yeulz estains,
Qui faisoient regars et ris,
Dont maintz marchans furent attains,
Nez courbé, de beaulte loingtains,
Oreilles pendans et moussues,
Le vis pally, mort et destains,
Menton foncé, joues peaussues:

"C'est d'humaine beaulté l'yssues!
Les bras courts et les mains contraictes,
Les espaulles toutes bossues,
Mammelles, quoy! toutes retraictes,
Telle les hanches que les tettes.
Du sadinet, fy! Quand des cuysses,
Cuysses ne sont plus, mais cuysettes
Grivelées comme saulcisses.

"Ainsi le bon temps regretons
Entre nous, povres vielles sottes,
Assises bas, à croppetons,
Tout en ung tas comme pelottes,
A petis feu de chenevottes,
Tost allumées, tost estainctes.
Et jadis fusmes se mignottes . . .
Ainsi emprend à maintz et maintes."

I thought I heard Belle Heaulmière
Lamenting for her long-lost youth,
Complaining to the earless air
In piteous words of bitter truth:
"You knave, you robber, age uncouth,
Who gave you right to lay me by?
What's left to stop me now, in sooth,
From seeking for a way to die?

"You've stolen from me the proud sway
To which my beauty gave me right
O'er every man who came my way:
Clerk, merchant, priest, all did delight
With Heaulmière to spend the night,
And gave their wealth to lie with me.
Now even tramps lack appetite
Enough to take this carcass free.

"Yet many a man did I deny
(Which wasn't very wise of me)
For love of one lad, smooth and sly,

Whom I supported royally,
Toadying to his every plea.
I loved him so I would have sold
My soul for him if needed be—
He only loved me for my gold.

"He treated me like meanest dirt,
Trod on my toes and kicked my rear,
And yet, he was a cunning flirt—
One kiss, one tender word I'd hear
And once again I would take cheer.
He got me pregnant, did me in;
My wages in that bitter year
Were degradation, shame, and sin.

"But twenty years ago he died.
Old, I remain, grizzled and gray,
To weep with time's receding tide,
Comparing now and yesterday.
I see my body waste away,
Dried up, distorted, ugly, thin;
And powerless such change to stay,
I rant and rage and fume within.

"Where is my brow so smooth and white,
My eyebrows arched, my golden hair,
My glorious eyes whose ardent light
In all men's hearts made passion flare?
Where is the face that made men stare?
My dimpled chin, my saucy nose,
My pointed ears, that pretty pair,
My lips, vermilion as a rose?

"Those shapely shoulders, gently plump,
Long arms and hands that moved with grace,
My little breasts, my rounded rump,
Pertly designed to fit its place
And make men gasp for my embrace;
My most desired, that garden small,
Which my strong thighs did tightly case,
Alas, my lures, where are you all?

"Eyebrows collapsed and eyes half blind,
Whose teasing once with laughter gay
Drove many a merchant from his mind;
Forehead wrinkled and hair turned gray,
A pasty face that fades away;
Lips of leather, ears moss-grown,
Pendulous nose—this foul decay
Is all that I can call my own. . . .

"This is the end of beauty's road:
These shortened arms and hands curled in,
These shoulders hunched like some old toad,
These sagging breasts and buttocks thin;
Thighs speckled as a sausage skin,
No meat inside to hold them taut.
Love? What man's love could I now win?
Ravaged, the garden all men sought.

"Here I sit with the other hags
All whining for the good old days,
Hunched like a bunch of half-filled bags,
Circled around a tiny blaze

Of oak twigs whose brief darting rays,
Quickly ignited, quickly done,
The story of our lives portrays—
And that of many another one."

Nor was Villon's insight limited to transgressors. This same poet who could see the story of la Belle Heaulmière's life through her eyes as she stared into the oak-twig fire could identify as well with his mother, the illiterate servant at the Abbey of the Celestins. He sensed her mute emotions and gave voice to the hopes she didn't dare express for a better life hereafter as keenly as he echoed la Belle Heaulmière's regrets for a life impossible to regain. Methodically, Villon twice inspected la Belle Heaulmière *toute nue,* brow to buttocks, in youth and age, giving us her own thoughts as she looked in the mirror. His mother he gave us on her knees before murals of saints and sinners on chapel walls. Though she couldn't read the prayers in the prayer book, she could learn by heart: if her son would write a prayer and teach her the lines, she would have her own prayer to repeat. And so he wrote the *Ballade pour Prier Nostre-Dame,* the Ballade to Pray to Our Lady, and here are some of the lines Villon's mother knelt to say:

Dame du ciel, regente terrienne,
Emperiere des infernaulx paluz,
Recevez-moy, vostre humble chrestienne:

Qui comprinse soye entre vos esleuz,
Ce non obstant qu'oncques rien ne valuz.
Les biens de vous, ma dame et ma maistresse,
Sont trop plus grans que ne suis pecheresse,
Sans lesquelz biens ame ne peult merir
N'avoir les cieulx. Je n'en suis menteresse:
En ceste foy je vueil vivre et mourir.

Femme je suis povrette et ancienne,
Qui riens ne sçay, oncques lettre ne leuz;
Au monstier voy dont suis paroissienne,
Paradis painct, où sont harpes et luz,
Et ung enfer où damnez sont boulluz;
L'ung me faict paour, l'autre joye et liesse.
La joye avoir fais-moy, haulte Deesse,
A qui pecheurs doivent tous recourir,
Comblez de foy, sans faincte ne paresse:
En ceste foy je vueil vivre et mourir.

Envoi

*V*ous portastes, Vierge, digne princesse,
*I*esus regnant, qui n'a ne fin ne cesse.
*L*e Tout-Puissant, prenant nostre foiblesse,
*L*aissa le cieulx et nous vint secourir,
*O*ffrist à mort sa tres chere jeunesse;
*N*ostre Seigneur est tel, je le confesse . . .
En ceste foy je vueil vivre et mourir.

Lady of Heaven, of earth the Queen,
Empress of Hell, receive my prayer.
Humble I am, unworthy have been

To be counted yours, your grace to share.
Yet, as a Christian, do I dare
To supplicate, for your mercies bide
Wider than my sins are wide.
All merits in those mercies lie;
High they are, as heaven is high:
And in this faith would I live and die.

Scant is the knowledge I can glean,
Who cannot read and have no share
Of worldly goods. But I have seen
Heaven on my church walls where
Harps and lutes are painted fair,
And hell, with sinners boiled and fried.
From hell in fright I try to hide,
In joy I look to heaven's sky
While offering my heartfelt prayer:
And in this faith would I live and die.

Envoi

*V*irgin, you were of God the Bride,
*I*n you our Saviour did abide.
*L*ord Jesus, you were crucified,
*L*iving among us, living on high,
*O*mnipotent yet human guide,
*N*ow King in whom we can confide:
And in this faith would I live and die.

Did Villon give this poem, with his signature in the
envoi, to his mother on some visit she may have made to

his bedside as he lay dictating to Fremin? We know that he wrote the poem at this time, including it in the *Grand Testament,* and that he wrote it at her specific request, for he subtitled it with the words: "Made by Villon at the Request of His Mother." But we do not know on what occasions the two got together. The Testament has other compassionate references to his mother, but no description of his personal relationship with her.

Those winter months of 1461 to 1462, during which most of his greatest poetry was written, finally gave way to spring. Ice broke on the rivers. The ducks of the Seine waddled, flap-happy, in its ditches. Barges moved. Seine-side markets, spare in the snows, began again to burst with fresh produce, the lovely little artichokes from Brittany, the savory cheeses, the ripe fruits, the feathery greens. And fish. The fish vendors on the Petit Pont, Villon's favorite bridge across the river, regained full voice, full swing, as they thumped their tubs or a customer's nose. In June, the bonfires burned in the Place de Grève and the flies swarmed back to the butcher stalls.

Ah, Paris. No matter how his companions of the road during his years of exile had boasted about their native provinces—peddlers and pilgrims from Toulouse and Gascony, Valence, Lorraine, and Picardy—against the lot he'd guarantee his Paris had the best of it.

Villon thawed with the rest of his city. He got out of bed. He went back to the Pomme de Pin. And after a tankard or two of the Beaune wine he loved with those of his old companions who were left, it was all too easy to slip back into his old habits. By autumn—on the third of November, 1462—he was in jail again, locked up in the Châtelet, charged with theft. Either he pilfered something of small value or he was wrongly accused, a frequent occurrence in his time; otherwise, he would not have been let out a couple of days later. He was about to leave the Châtelet when Laurence Poutrel, that Saint Benoît clergyman and dean of Navarre College who had always dogged his steps, caught up with him once more. Poutrel, examining a list of Châtelet prisoners ready for release, spotted Villon's name. He promptly paid a fee amounting to sixteen cents to register opposition to freeing Villon. Villon was detained, and Poutrel brought up the Navarre robbery charge. He demanded that Villon repay fifty gold pieces, as the other thieves had been forced to do.

Of course Villon had no gold. He sent a message to his uncle, who paid. Freed from jail on November 7, Villon returned to his room in the Porte Rouge at Saint Benoît.

During all his short life, the pre-Christmas season seemed to be the time when François Villon got into the most trouble. In 1452, it had been the affair of the Pet-au-Diable; in 1456, the Navarre robbery; in 1460, the theft of the chalice which led to his being thrown into Thibaud d'Aussigny's Meung dungeon. Of his recorded conflicts with the law, only the stabbing of the priest Sermoise happened out of season, so to speak, and of that affair Villon had not been the initiator. If Villon was aware of this coincidence, small wonder he insisted that he was "limited to what must be by stars' design."

The year 1462 brought no exception to his season of ill fortune. On December 7, Robin Dogis, proprietor of the Mule Tavern in the Rue Saint Jacques, not far from Saint Benoît, invited Villon and two mutual friends, Mutin de Moustier and Rogier Pichart, to have a free meal at the tavern. After dinner, Villon invited Dogis and the others to spend the evening at the Porte Rouge. Slightly tipsy from the wine which the hospitable Dogis had poured freely, the four men skidded their way on foot along the icy street toward Villon's room. They passed the office of François Ferrebouc, the Saint Benoît lawyer who had been appointed to serve on the jury for the exoneration of Joan of Arc. During Villon's absence, Ferrebouc had also been made a papal notary. He now had a large office, and several clerks working for him.

On this night the clerks were working late. It was about eight o'clock, an hour before curfew, and the light of many candles, perched on the clerks' desks, gleamed through the casement windows. One window stood slightly ajar. Pichart spit through it. His companions shouted jeers at the industry of the young men plugging away at their papers. Stung, several of the clerks bounded from the office, one of them yelling, "What sort of rowdy drunks are you?" They grabbed Mutin de Moustier, who stood nearest the door, and dragged him inside, he shouting lustily, *"Au meutre! On me tue! Je suis mort!"* Murder! I'm being killed! I'm dead!

Ferrebouc had been sleeping. Awakened by the racket, he threw a fur cape over his shoulders and rushed into the street, in his hurry knocking down Dogis. Dogis drew his dagger and slashed at Ferrebouc, wounding him slightly.

Villon claimed to have taken no part in the affair, in fact to have left the scene as soon as Ferrebouc appeared. He was doubtless telling the truth, for he respected Ferrebouc greatly. But Ferrebouc gave Villon's name to the police, along with the names of the others. Villon, Dogis, and Pichart were condemned to be hanged. Moustier, for some unknown reason, got off with a term in prison. Although the punishment seems out of proportion to the crime, such disproportion was typical of Paris and much of France in Villon's day. It was the law-and-order reaction to the social chaos that came out of the Hundred Years' War.

Villon appealed his sentence and, poet even at the point of death, wrote the appeal in the form of a ballade. His uncle made every conceivable effort to have the sentence softened. Despite these attempts, however, Villon was by no means sure of leniency. In his cell in the Châtelet he could almost feel around his scrawny neck the noose which

had so recently broken the necks of Colin de Cayeux and
René de Montigny. Having dispatched his appeal, he wrote
another ballade, the one perhaps most quoted, most translated, and most admired of all his work, *L'Epitaphe de
Villon,* sometimes called the Ballade of the Hanged. Addressed to his *frères humains,* his fellow men, it begs them
in all charity to pray for victims of the Paris gallows and to
take care to avoid a like end themselves. He concludes:

> La pluie nous a bués et lavés,
> Et le soleil desséchés et noircis;
> Pies, corbeaux, nous ont les yeux cavés,
> Et arraché la barbe et les sourcils.
> Jamais nul temps nous ne sommes assis;
> Puis ça, puis la, comme le vent varie,
> A son plaisir sans cesser nous charrie,
> Plus becquetés d'oiseaux que dés a coudre.
> Ne soyez donc de notre confrerie;
> Mais priez Dieu que tous nous veuille absoudre!

> Prince Jesus, qui sur tous a maîtrie,
> Garde qu'Enfer n'ait de nous seigneurie:
> A lui n'ayons que faire ne que soudre.
> Hommes, ici n'a point de moquerie;
> Mais priez Dieu que tous nous veuille absoudre!

> Rain-scoured as by a purgative,
> Sun-dried and blackened as by blight,
> To magpies, crows, our bodies give

A superwhetted appetite—
Their needle beaks in our eyes delight,
Never we sit, never recline,
But ever swing as the wind shifts line;
Scudded like clouds, first here, then there.
Let us be a lesson to thee and thine,
And offer to God for us a prayer.

Lord Jesus, all powers, all worlds are thine.
Lest Hell for eternity confine
Our souls, deliver us from its snare.
Men, make no mock, though we swing like swine:
But offer to God instead your prayer.

The epitaph was premature. On January 5, 1463, the highest court of the land, to which Villon and his uncle had succeeded in getting his case transferred, commuted the death sentence. But the sentence they substituted, "in view of the evil life of the said Villon," was for Villon merely another form of death. Banishment from Paris. For ten years, beginning immediately. For that length of time, to set foot in the city or any of its suburbs would mean instant loss of life.

In another ballade, Villon asked for three days' grace to say farewells and gather together what money he might. He knew very well that his existence in banishment would be more rigorous, more precarious than any even he had ever experienced. His previous exiles had been voluntary. Although he had not cared for it, the open road had been his by right. This time he would be regarded as a rebel, a man to be shunned. No free hospice would take him in. Precious little companionship would mellow his journeys. Even the church was not allowed to help him, as he was considered the property of the king. This was the law of banishment.

His request for a three-day postponement was granted. At the end of it, on January 8, 1463, at the age of thirty-two, he left Paris. Four years later, in 1467, the population of Paris had been so diminished by war and epidemics that Louis XI, in order to repopulate the city, issued an edict of pardon for banishees and escaped criminals. All crimes except treason were forgiven. Villon was free to return. But he did not. It is inconceivable that he would have stayed away had he still been alive. Kings' pardons were well publicized. Villon, alive, would certainly have known of this one and would have found means, as he had done before, to get himself back to the city which was his world. The death in whose shadow he had lived had almost certainly found him before 1467.

But though Villon had vanished in the flesh, his spirit grew larger than life. The first complete edition of his works appeared almost with the dawn of European printing, in Paris, in 1489. By 1532, nineteen more editions had been printed. And not only his poetry lived on. Almost as soon as he disappeared, the man himself became a legend. Tales of his wining, his love-making, his rapscallion adventures multiplied and were embellished in the multiplication. In 1500 many of these legends were published in a volume called *Les Repues Franches,* Free Meals, a collection of tales in rhyme purporting to reveal the exploits of Villon as an expert thief of fish, tripe, bread, and wine. The book was a best-seller.

This legendary Villon, hero of the Repues Franches and of tale tellers at country fairs, was, however, an entirely different person from the Villon revealed in the poet's own verses. The mythical man was held up as a model for thieves, a man clever enough to get away with his crimes. The real Villon, admittedly a thief, was forever cautioning other thieves to give up their unsavory profession, forever regretting that he himself had joined it. The legendary Villon was a gay, handsome blade, a devil-may-care buccaneer. The real Villon, as one of his poems plainly tells us, resembled a turnip. Though he had his moments of gaiety, it was a gaiety tinged with irony, a humor that bit rather than roared. And he was far from devil-may-care, the true Villon, wondering most of his adult life where his next meal would come from.

Not until 1533 was a more lifelike image of Villon displayed to public view. Clément Marot, a sensitive young poet at the court of France's first resplendent Renaissance king, Francis I, edited a volume of Villon's poetry in which he deleted spurious material that had crept from legend into the poems themselves. In an introduction, he drew a portrait of the poet which restored Villon to Villon and to France.

Marot was himself a rebel who, like Villon, suffered exile and jail, although Marot's rebellion was of a totally different nature from Villon's. He was among the Renaissance thinkers who questioned and protested certain doctrines of the Roman Catholic Church—in other words, a Protestant. He delighted in translating into everyday French the Psalms then printed only in church Latin, an act which was condemned as heresy.

Heretic or no, his edition of Villon was well received by Renaissance readers. They were avid for the realism which had placed Villon so far ahead of his time. Marot, for whom Villon, above all fifteenth-century poets, deserved, as he put it, "the crown of laurels," regretted that Villon had not lived in the sixteenth century instead. "Surely," Marot wrote, "he too would have been taken in at court. He would have been supported in comfort. He could have written much more."

Marot's judgment on this score is debatable. Would Villon have been so well able to interpret the suffering and yearning he saw around him, had he not shared it? While living in luxury at the court of Charles d'Orléans, he himself referred in his prize-winning ballade to "the riches that lose everything." At the end of his *Grand Testament,* he wrote an epitaph for himself which was also in a sense an epitaph for Coquillards like Colin and René, illiterate scrubwomen like his mother, foolish *filles de joie* like la Belle

Heaulmière, beggars contemplating suicide, and all the other outcasts who were his legatees and whom he regarded as his brothers and sisters:

> Repos eternel donne a cil,
> Sire, et clarté perpetuelle,
> Qui vaillant plat ni écuelle
> N'ot oncques, n'un brin de persil.
> Il fut res, chef, barbe et sourcil,
> Comme un navet qu'on ret ou pele.
> Repos eternel donne a cil.
>
> Rigueur le transmit en exil
> Et lui frappa au cil la pelle,
> Non obstant qu'il dît: "J'en appelle!"
> Qui n'est pas terme trop subtil.
> Repos eternel donne a cil.
>
> God's peace eternal may he feel
> In light of heaven's unending day,
> Who bowl, nor plate nor parsley spray
> Could call his own to serve a meal.
> Though bald as turnip housemaids peel—
> Hair, beard, and eyebrows scraped away—
> God's peace eternal may he feel.
>
> Harsh fate a shovel's blow did deal
> His buttocks, heaving him away
> To exile, though he fought to stay,
> Protesting loudly, "I appeal!"
> God's peace eternal may he feel.

Could a bewigged François Villon, placidly eating from the gold and silver plates which Francis favored, have written this rondel? Says André Mary, a modern authority on Villon: "When he left Paris, never to return, he had accomplished his destiny; he had cried his cry. One cannot see how he could have added anything to it. He was one of those quickly maturing geniuses who exhaust their talents in one stunning moment of time, burning out their lives."

CHAPTER VI

Across the Centuries

The refusal to let Villon die has persisted from his time to ours. That his poetry lived on, not only in French, but translated into English, German, Italian, Czech, and Russian, isn't surprising. Art is eternal. But rarely does the personality of the artist himself arouse the continuing curiosity, conjecture, and debate that François Villon has excited for more than five hundred years. Age to age, all sorts of creative people—poets, novelists, playwrights, musicians—have found in Villon the man inspiration for their own fancies.

Some of these fancies have taken the form of trying to imagine what happened to Villon after he left Paris in 1463. The first of these projections was written by a contemporary of Marot's who shared Marot's interest in Villon, François Rabelais. He resurrected the poet, alive and well, in Belgium, Poitou, and finally in England at the court of Edward V. Rabelais, a man with a gift for uproarious mockery, had in common with Villon a hatred of pretension. In his best-known works, stories of a rollicking, roistering giant whom he called Gargantua, and the giant's son, Pantagruel, he exposed to ridicule whatever he saw as artificial in the Renaissance Establishment. His books, frequently bawdy, were banned—but still, King Francis had them read to him at meals. Listening to the adventures of Pantagruel, Francis would have met Villon in several sequences—a Villon as ribald as Rabelais himself, but without the sympathy which gave Villon's ribaldry its cutting edge, its point.

Rabelais' reference to Villon in Belgium is brief, but in the Poitevin village of Saint Maixent, of which he makes Villon a resident, he spins a long tale about the poet's pranks. In it, Villon writes and produces a religious pageant for the community. To costume players, he seeks to borrow some robes from a local friar. The friar refuses. Villon determines to get revenge. After the pageant, he and several others, still dressed for the devils' roles which they had played, surprise the friar, riding to his monastery on his mare. The devils wave long forks, well charred from the bake oven whose proprietor had loaned them. They carry smoking torches, and in the bleary light they set off flares. The friar's mare rears in fright, half throwing its rider, and takes to a gallop. The friar, one foot caught in a stirrup, is dragged behind, through woods and ditches and over hedgerows, "in one long carnage," according to Rabelais. The hapless rider is completely dismembered. The mare shows up at the monastery with all that is left of the friar—one foot dangling in the stirrup.

Though Rabelais' tale of Villon in Poitou was popular

Renaissance reading, his view of the poet is at odds with both logic and history. It is highly unlikely that Villon, who, as far as we know, drew his own dagger only in self-defense, would have permitted another human being to be dragged, dismembered, to his death.

In time, the conjecture that Villon settled in Poitou after his banishment gained a certain amount of credence with some of his biographers. It also formed the basis for several modern novels. Two of these, *The Brief Hour of François Villon* by John Erskine, and *Needles and Pins* by Justin Huntly McCarthy, are remarkable for the skill with which their authors bring to life the kind of person who could have written Villon's poetry.

John Erskine was a man of many talents. New York City born, a professor of English, first at Amherst College, then at his alma mater, Columbia University, he was distinguished for his books of literary criticism and history. He was also a gifted concert pianist, for nine years president of the Juilliard School of Music in New York. He was best known to the public, however, for his historical novels, a succession of which were published in the first half of the twentieth century. *The Brief Hour of François Villon* was one of these.

In a short foreword, Erskine gives us his estimate of the man: "He mourned the briefness of time. Beauty filled his eyes, he would miss none of it, and in his haste he stumbled, which brings his story home to you and me. He painted

himself in dark colors, yet the portrait survives. More than
badness went into the fabric of his immortality . . . To
live bravely, in his fashion, is a step up toward goodness."
In this spirit, Erskine weaves a tale about a Villon who
continued to ascend the ladder of goodness. He has a
daughter by Catherine de Vaucelles and brings the child
with him to Saint Maixent. He makes his living in the
village by tutoring the son of the apothecary. The two children grow up and marry each other. The book is less a
novel than it is a collection of short stories about Villon, the
philosopher of Saint Maixent, his tender relationship with
his daughter and his love affair with a woman who dies in
the end. Erskine precedes each of these quiet episodes with
a translation of an appropriate poem of Villon's.

By contrast, McCarthy's *Needles and Pins* is the story of
a man of action. Every chapter is loud with duels, head-
bashings, ambushes, and uprisings. The author, an Irish
historian, novelist, and playwright of the late nineteenth
and early twentieth centuries, was as versed in French as in
English. He had translated a good many French novels before he wrote of Villon, a subject which was to intrigue him
through two novels and a drama.

In *Needles and Pins,* Villon marries Catherine de Vaucelles and goes to live with her on an estate that she has
inherited in Poitou. The couple are not welcomed by their
neighbors, noblemen who resent newcomers and look down
their noses at Catherine's marriage to a commoner. The

leader of the non-welcome committee is one Gontier de Grigny, fat, red-faced, and disagreeable. McCarthy constructs this character from two others in Villon's poetry. One is the Seigneur de Grigny, a man known for his inability to get along with his neighbors and his tendency to violent quarrels. In the *Grand Testament,* Villon left him a powder keg; in the *Petit Testament,* some fierce dogs. The second person is the rustic writer whose ideals of romance Villon ridiculed in the poem that gave us the realistic portrait of the fat priest and his girlfriend making love in a room "cozy with tapestry."

McCarthy's combining of these two persons into a new character is a type of license many authors have taken in fiction about Villon. As the novel continues, Villon gives a third name to Gontier: he nicknames him "Bullface." Bullface has Villon hanged in effigy. He persuades the congregation in the local church to refuse to sit near Villon and Catherine. Villon ambushes Bullface, drags him from his horse, and trusses him up in a rope sling on the gibbet where Bullface had hanged the effigy of Villon. Then Villon gets word to Paris that on a certain Sunday the Poitevin church will sponsor a generous almsgiving. All the rabble of Paris make haste to be there. They are instructed by Villon to fill the church, except for space around Catherine and Villon's seats. When the haughty nobles arrive, their choice is to sit near the couple—or remain standing. After the service Villon dons the robe of a friar and preaches a sermon on the church steps, prior to the distribution of alms. In this sermon McCarthy reflects the social philosophy which pervaded Villon's poetry as well as the depth of the poet's religious conviction. While today's reader may find much of *Needles and Pins* too sentimental and too blustering for his taste, the sermon McCarthy put on the lips of his Villon is as relevant in spirit now as when Villon himself rhymed similar beliefs:

"The Kingdom of God is like unto a lazar-house* set upon the shores of a sea, and in every room there are many beds, clean and warm and smelling of wholesome herbs. Over the sea . . . many vessels ply to and fro through the ages, without pause. Those that come are heavy with their burden of the wretched, that are indeed the children of God: the halt . . . the blind and the misshapen . . . lepers and plague-stricken . . . those that are stained by sores and eaten by ulcers . . . those that rot while they still live . . . these are the creatures that are carried over the sea to the lazar-house of God.

"And in that house . . . angels go up and down, and there is healing in their touch and healing in their speech which is the speech that is spoken in the courts of heaven, and there is healing . . . in the rustle of their wings. And one by one these miserables are made whole, even as they

* Medieval term for a hospital for leprosy or other disfiguring and contagious diseases.

should seem if the world were what the world is not
yet . . .

"Comrades, remember there is a kingdom of earth as
well as a kingdom of heaven . . . Earth can never be
made like unto heaven, but earth can be made less like unto
hell. I think there shall come a time when men that suffer
and . . . weep, those that are oppressed and . . . re-
jected shall share honestly in the world's pleasure, as they
now share dishonestly . . . in the world's pains. Not always will the power and the glory lie in the hands of a few.
Not always shall the many toil and hunger and mourn that
the few may take their ease and feast and be merry. In the
age of . . . wisdom, which is the age of humanity, which
is the age of Christ recognized, there will be neither masters
nor slaves, but men."

The sermon is so anti-Establishment that even Catherine
takes exception to it. The couple quarrel. The breach widens
when Villon frees two thieves caught poaching on their
estate. When he welcomes five of his old Pomme de Pin
gang to the manor, Catherine's irritation deepens to fury;
she withdraws to her own part of the castle. We are following a familiar plot pattern now: boy having won girl, boy
and girl split. Predictably, the next scene introduces the
triangle, a rival for Catherine—a young woman on a neigh-
boring estate who turns out to be the illegitimate daughter

of Louis XI. In the end, Catherine and Villon are of course reunited, but not until McCarthy has given us some lively history. He has Louis XI appoint Villon his lieutenant for Poitou, and as such Villon is engaged to some degree in the reunification of France which that monarch achieved at the end of the century of war that had split the country apart.

Another interesting facet of this book is the poetry which McCarthy puts on Villon's lips at every turn. It is not Villon's poetry; it is McCarthy's. But one has to admire the skill with which McCarthy was able to make his character react in rhyme. The verses say precisely what one would expect François Villon to say if confronted with the situations with which McCarthy confronts him, and they say it with Villonesque deftness.

McCarthy, Rabelais, and John Erskine were the major fabricators of a new life for Villon after banishment. In the centuries that separated Rabelais' crudities from Erskine's reverie and McCarthy's swashbuckling, Villon had continued to be read. It was not until the nineteenth century, however, that he became an artistic vogue.

The vogue began in the middle of the century in England, among a group of poets, painters, writers, and designers known as Pre-Raphaelites. Their aim was to do away with artificiality in their work—to let it present the primitive in man and nature. They looked for inspiration to Italian artists who had preceded the famous painter, Raphael.

The poets and writers among them were noted for their presentations of the sensuous. This group organized a Villon Society, for which the first English translations of Villon's poetry were made, by an American dramatist, John Howard Payne, who had settled in England, making his living by translating French plays for the English stage. Shortly afterward, a leading Pre-Raphaelite, the painter-poet Dante Gabriel Rossetti, and another poet who was a close friend of Rossetti's, Algernon Charles Swinburne, also turned their talents to translating Villon.

The Pre-Raphaelites' motivation was in large part anti-Victorianism. From early childhood, they had been reared according to the standards of Queen Victoria, the exceedingly proper matron who then occupied the British throne. Her Majesty not only reigned within constitutional limitations, she strongly influenced the morals of her countrymen. Her stringent code of behavior included taboos on the display or mention of any part of the human torso between shoulders and ankles, as well as any reference to the body's functions. So the Pre-Raphaelites painted nudes and wrote of sexual love. They were the artistic wing—and to some extent the advance heralds—of a revolt against Victorianism, which began after a quarter century of acceptance of the queen's prohibitions. Outward acceptance, that is. The prostitutes of Victorian England, though less flagrant than la Belle Heaulmière and her sisterhood, were just as busy.

Villon's frankness and sincerity, his disregard of convention for convention's sake, his contempt for hypocrisy, all appealed to the Pre-Raphaelites. And because they lived in an age of surface morality not only in sexual relationships but in politics and economics as well, they were equally attracted by Villon's denunciation of oppression. Oppression was a commonplace in their time, too, brought on by what is now called the Industrial Revolution. The invention of the steam engine and spinning and weaving machines in the previous century had given rise to a multiplicity of manufacturing concerns. The individual artisan couldn't compete with the output of a factory. He had little choice except to shut up shop and go to work for men who had the capital to buy the new machines—at whatever wage the owners set.

Some of the Pre-Raphaelites' fathers were among the portly rich who sat on the boards of directors of the factories, growing richer by exploiting their workers. These workers, men, women, and children alike, labored long hours, for low pay, often under hazardous conditions. Raw materials to feed the machines at which they toiled came from colonies which British regiments had been subjugating, one after the other, from the tip of Africa to the slopes of the Himalayas. And propping up this social system was a law-and-order code of almost barbaric severity. It listed more than two hundred offenses punishable by death. Prisons were hardly preferable to death. They were houses of vengeance where murderers, rapists, perverts, debtors, sheep thieves, shoplifters, gyp artists, and child fruit-filchers were dumped together, regardless of sex, in cells without sanitation.

Thanks to the outcry of writers and the efforts of reformers, most of these injustices were on the way to correction before the end of Victoria's reign. But during the years when the Pre-Raphaelites were growing up, many a verse of Villon's would have had a familiar ring. The driven thief, the suicidal beggar, the spent servant woman, the destitute and aging *fille-de-joie,* the hungry staring at bread they couldn't afford, the Meung dungeon, the hangman who broke necks with glee—these were portraits the Pre-Raphaelites could recognize.

Not only the content but the style of Villon's poems attracted them, particularly his use of the medieval ballade and rondel. In their search for simplicity, they had settled on the Middle Ages as the period supplying, to their taste, the most exquisite forms. One of them, William Morris, wrote two treatises explaining why: he called them *News from Nowhere* and *The Dream of John Ball.* They drew sharp contrasts between Morris' machine world and the quality of medieval art. Morris was the most versatile of the versatile Pre-Raphaelites. He was poet, painter, writer, architect, designer of furniture and stained glass, and an active reformer who founded the Socialist League. He was also an avid Villon reader. Politically, artistically, and emotionally,

Villon was for Morris and his fellow artists the model of a
master poet. Swinburne summed up their admiration in his
Ballade of François Villon, Prince of All Ballade-Makers.

Bird of the bitter bright gray golden morn,
    Scarce risen upon the dusk of dolorous years,
First of us all and sweetest singer born,
    Whose far shrill note the world of new men hears
    Cleave the cold shuddering shade as twilight clears;
When song new-born put off the old world's attire
And felt its tune on her changed lips expire,
    Writ foremost on the roll of them that came
Fresh girt for service of the latter lyre,
    Villon, our sad bad glad mad brother's name!

Alas the joy, the sorrow and the scorn
    That clothed thy life with hopes and sins and fears,
And gave thee stones for bread and tares for corn,
    And plume-plucked gaol-birds for thy starveling peers,
    Till death clipt close their flight with shameful shears;
Till shifts came short and loves were hard to hire,
When lilt of song nor twitch of twangling wire
    Would buy thee bread or kisses; when light fame
Spurned like a ball and haled through brake and briar,
    Villon, our sad bad glad mad brother's name!

Poor splendid wings so frayed and soiled and torn!
    Poor kind wild eyes so dashed with light quick tears!
Poor perfect voice, most blithe when most forlorn,
    That rings athwart the sea whence no man steers
    Like joy-bells crossed with death-bells in our ears!

What far delight has cooled the fierce desire
That like some ravenous bird was strong to tire
    On that frail flesh and soul consumed with flame,
But left more sweet than roses to respire;
    Villon, our sad bad glad mad brother's name?

Envoi

Prince of sweet songs made out of tears and fire,
A harlot was thy nurse, a God thy sire,
    Shame soiled thy song and song assailed thy shame,
But from thy feet now death has washed the mire,
Love reads out first and head of all our quire,
    Villon, our sad bad glad mad brother's name.

Swinburne, Rossetti, and John Payne, among the three of them, translated into English a major portion of Villon's poetry. The translations first appeared in *The Germ,* a magazine the Pre-Raphaelites published with the intent of stimulating interest in their views. Reading the poems, other English writers woke up to Villon. The poet William Ernest Henley did a spirited job of reproducing in a dialect of English thieves the gist of Villon's *Good Advice to Those of Evil Life*. With the title *Villon's Straight Tip to All Cross Coves* (young crooks), Henley began:

    Suppose you screeve? or go cheap-jack?
        Or fake the broads? or fig a nag?
    Or thimble-rig? or knap a yack?
        Or pitch a snide? or smash a rag?

> Suppose you duff? or nose and lag?
> Or get the straight and land your pot?
> How do you melt the multy swag?
> Booze and blowens cop the lot.

In plain English, the stanza says:

Suppose you beg, or huckster fake goods, or counterfeit coins, or cheat at horse trading, at cards, at dice, or at coin-flipping; suppose you forge documents, steal, or get paid off for squealing to the police, or rig a poker game to win the pot? How do you spend the loot? Liquor and women take it all.

This lighthearted transposition horrified one of Henley's best friends, that accomplished author of adventure stories, travel tales, and poetry, Robert Louis Stevenson. Henley and Stevenson had collaborated in the writing of several dramas, but Villon nearly broke up their partnership. Stevenson, Victorian to the bone, saw Villon as "a scoundrel, a liar, a thief, a moral degenerate whose eyes were sealed with his own filth." In the beginning of his short biography of Villon, entitled *François Villon, Student, Poet and Housebreaker*, Stevenson says, "For a man who is greedy of all pleasures and provided with little money and less dignity of character, we may prophesy a safe and speedy voyage downward." He fulfills his own prophecy at the end with the conclusion that Villon is "certainly the sorriest figure on the rolls of fame." In the pages between, he bulwarks his foregone conclusion with obtuse misreadings of what Villon was trying to say, interspersed with ser- monettes. Stevenson misinterprets Villon's compassion for the poor as "envy of the rich," calling the poet's thesis that poverty drives men to steal "a calumny on the noble army of the poor," and adding, "Every morning's sun sees thou- sands who pass, whistling, to their toil."

Where, one wonders, was the young Stevenson in July of 1866, when this noble army of whistlers knocked down the lampposts of London and set fire to the gas pipes beneath in protest against working and living conditions? Where was he when they repeated the performance in the manufactur- ing town of Birmingham two years later? Where, in the 1880's, when the *Bitter Cry of Outcast London,* a report by a group of clergymen on the horrors of slum life, electrified even the Parliament and the queen?

Apparently indifferent to conditions which were alarm- ing his own contemporaries, Stevenson was equally unmoved by Villon's pleas for the oppressed of the Middle Ages. In Villon's compassion for prostitutes, Stevenson sees only vice. He finds the aged Heaulmière "gross" and "grimy." Ever etiquette-conscious, he condemns Villon's "To hell with love like yours, Vaucelles," as an "ungentlemanly attitude." Of Villon himself he says, "The wolf and the pig struggled together in his face." Since the only picture we have of Villon is his own word picture in his poetry, which of course says nothing of the sort, Stevenson's description is, to say the least, open to question.

The wolf-pig description occurs in a short story, *Lodging for the Night,* which Stevenson based on one of the discredited *Repues Franches* legends. In it, Villon begs a meal, and after his host has served him, given him lodging, and retired, Villon repays the kindness by stealing everything worthwhile in the house. However, in this tale Stevenson the writer gets the better of Stevenson the preacher. He caught the spirit of Villon's Paris on a cold winter night:

The whole city was sleeted up. If there were any belated birds in heaven, they saw the island like a large white patch and the bridges like slim white spars on the black ground of the river. High overhead the snow settled among the tracery of the cathedral towers. Many a niche was drifted full; many a statue wore a long white bonnet on its grotesque or sainted head.

He goes on to have Villon say, passing the frozen corpse of a prostitute and shuddering at the howl of a wolf:

"This is a hard world in winter for wolves and wenches and poor rogues like me."

Having ended up by presenting a sympathetic character in spite of himself, Stevenson later commented in annoyance that the story "strikes me as much too picturesque by half!"

Still, in spite of his stiff-necked disapproval of Villon the man, he was unable to resist admiring Villon the poet. "This gallows bird was the great writer of his age and country, and initiated modern literature for France," he admitted in a tone of some astonishment. He added: "The old author breaking with *éclat de voix* out of his tongue-tied century has not yet been touched on his own ground and still gives us the most vivid and shocking impression of reality. The pleasure we take in the author's skill repays us . . . for the baseness of his attitude."

Stevenson's fascination with Villon's poetry led him to translate the *Grand Testament,* but the translation was no service to readers. He frequently omitted lines, sometimes whole passages, if he considered them in bad taste. One can readily believe that his inhibitions made translation difficult for him. He would not have considered weighing down his own poetry with archaic expressions like "eyne" for eyes, or "Methought erewhile," or "Think on't," with which he managed to rob Villon of the very modernity he admired.

Moreover, a good many of Stevenson's translations don't even say what Villon said. It is almost never possible to transpose literally and simultaneously from one tongue to another the meaning, rhyme, and rhythm of poetry, but to translate *les neiges d'antan* as "yesterday's snow" is stretching the figurative pretty far. *Antan* means long ago, of former times, nothing so close as yesterday. Much more deft is Rossetti's translation: "Where are the snows of yesteryear?'' In fact, Rossetti's expression is so apt that ''yester-year'' has found its way as a definition of *antan* into Cassell's classic French-English dictionary! To savor the difference between the two poets' interpretations, compare their handling of this quatrain from the *Ballade of Women of Former Times:*

VILLON:

> Echo parlant quand bruyt on maine
> Dessus rivière ou sus estan,
> Qui beaulté eut trop plus qu'humaine?
> Mais où sont les neiges d'antan?

STEVENSON:

> And Echo more than mortal fair
> That when one calls by river flow
> Or marish, answers out of air,
> But what has become of yesterday's snows?

ROSSETTI:

> Where is echo, beheld of no man,
> Only heard on river and mere—
> She whose beauty was more than human?
> But where are the snows of yesteryear?

In the second half of the nineteenth century the Villon vogue in which even Stevenson had found himself entangled passed from England back to France. Villon became the idol of a group of poets, way-out for their time, who were known as Symbolists. Some of them were friends of Pre-Raphaelites; all were admired by that group of English artists. Stevenson called the Symbolists ''literary perverts.'' They tended to be non-conformists in their life style as well as in their subject matter; invariably they were non-conforming in their poetic style. Like the Pre-Raphaelites, they were engaged in the search for the elemental, but their method of presenting it was much more complex. Believing that the basic nature of things could best be understood through the senses, they attempted to stimulate all the senses of their readers simultaneously. They filled their lines with intertwined images of elusive sound and scent, color, taste, and texture, blurring distinctions between senses. Thus, the most important of Symbolism's founders, Charles Baudelaire, could write of the *sound* of perfume and color:

Comme des long échos qui de loin se confondent
Les parfums, les couleurs et les sons se repondent . . .

Like long echoes that in distance confound,
Perfumes, colors, and sounds resound . . .

Baudelaire considered himself the spiritual heir of Villon, whom he called "the first and foremost poet of the wretched." Like Villon, Baudelaire was an urban poet, a poet of Paris. Also like Villon, he was the poet of Paris' seamy side. The city he evoked was the city of aged street vendors, beggars, thieves, and prostitutes. His literary philosophy was that beauty could be extracted from evil. His best collection of verses, *Les Fleurs du Mal (Flowers of*

Evil), based on this philosophy, outraged the smooth side of Paris. Baudelaire was fined for having written it. Nonchalant, he paid the fine and published three more editions of *Fleurs du Mal,* enriched by additional poems.

Typical of what incensed upper-strata Parisians in Baudelaire's view of their city are a pair of poems called *Dusk of Dawn* and *Dusk of Evening.* Both owe a deep debt to Villon's vision of Parisian subculture. Four hundred years later, Baudelaire's Paris was an updated reincarnation of Villon's. In *Dusk of Evening* he speaks of thieves who force cash registers in order to live for a few days and clothe their mistresses, and of prostitutes who "creep into the streets as though opening secret paths from an anthill." In dusky dawn, these same prostitutes, "with swollen eyelids and mouths agape, sleep the sleep of the exhausted." And

> L'aurore grelottante en robe rose et verte
> S'avançait lentement sur la Seine déserte,
> Et le sombre Paris, en se frottant les yeux,
> Empoignait ses outils, vieillard laborieux.

> The tremulous dawn in green and rose
> Lightens the path the forsaken Seine flows,
> While Paris in gray, rubbing its eyes,
> Grasps tools, an old worker preparing to rise.

Not only poets like Baudelaire, but painters and musicians too shared Symbolist ideals in art. Those who worked with canvas and keyboard called themselves Impressionists. The leading composer of Impressionist music was Claude Achille Debussy. He believed that "a musician should mix tones as a painter mixes hues." One of his own compositions, a nocturne, he described as "luminous dusk participating in total rhythm." To achieve the effect of mixed media, Debussy modulated—that is, changed the key in which he was composing—sometimes as often as every other beat. His music echoed the chants of the Middle Ages, the same period which fascinated the Pre-Raphaelite poets. Like medieval musicians, Debussy wrote mainly monophonic music—that is, melody without chords. He let the melody wander the musical staff at will, interspersing it with a great deal of dissonance. These techniques broke every rule in the book of the music critics of his time, and they called him a musical anarchist. No longer does this opinion hold. André Suarès, one of the most prominent modern French music critics, has dubbed Debussy "Claude de France, the most musical of the French, the most French of musicians."

Essentially a mood musician, Debussy was charmed by mood poetry. He set to music several of the poems of Symbolist and Pre-Raphaelite friends, some of Charles d'Orléans, and, toward the end of his life, three of Villon's ballades. It was not only Villon's moods which fascinated Debussy, however. He was, like Villon, a contender against man's exploitation of man. Unable to support himself by composing unconventional music, he eked out a living for some years as a journalist, writing unconventional articles about the evils of French colonialism in Africa.

Debussy lived long enough to see his music well accepted by the generation maturing at the beginning of the twentieth century. The century was eleven years old when a popular French singer, Paul Lestang, introduced at a concert Debussy's setting of Villon's ballade for his mother, his ballade for the women of Paris, and the ballade for his beloved, Marthe.

Debussy's accompaniment for the ballade for Marthe makes it into one long question mark. Piercing notes cry why, why, why: Why do you not love me? Why will you not succor me, love, before I die? When the song reaches the passage where Villon warns that age comes all too soon, the warning, beginning with *Un temps viendra*—a time will come—groans downhill like a record player grinding to a halt in a power failure. The rest of the stanza is distant thunder threatening a spring day. At the end, the *envoi* is resigned. Lestang's audience wiped their eyes.

Suddenly, they chuckled. *Il n'y a bon bec que de Paris,* affirmed Lestang in staccato tones. Buzz, buzz, echoed his accompanist in rapid-fire sixteenth notes. For each language mentioned in the *Ballade of the Women of Paris,* Debussy supplied a different tonal quality. Near melody for Bretons, drum rolls for Germans, guitar twangs for Spanish, lilt for Italians. And after all the others, the emphatic *envoi,* reasserting *Il n'y a bon bec que de Paris.*

The ballade for Villon's mother is almost a hymn. It opens with the piano tolling like slow bells. The rest is repetitive chanting of a plaintive tune. One can believe that Villon's mother would have had no trouble learning it by rote.

When Lestang introduced these ballades, they drowned out the rest of the evening's repertoire. The newspapers the next day were concerned only with Villon and Debussy. As one reviewer put it, "Poet and musician clasped hands across the centuries to achieve a perfect union of sound and meaning."

In the same season that the ballades were winning applause in Paris, the curtain was rising nightly on the stage of the Garden Theater in New York City on a scene laid in Villon's Pomme de Pin. The play was Justin Huntly McCarthy's *If I Were King*. It was in its tenth year at the Garden Theater and was to continue for five more years in theaters throughout the United States and England. In the role of François Villon for much of this time was the famous American actor, E. H. Sothern. On opening night, December 1, 1901, the audience was on its feet, cheering, long before the play was over. Sothern was forced to step out of his part long enough to acknowledge the reception before he could go on. Next morning a review in the *New York World* declared: "It was a winning night for Justin Huntly McCarthy, E. H. Sothern and François Villon. The triumvirate have brought us a play that sparkles." The reception was the same wherever the sixty-eight actors in the cast traveled throughout the country in their private train.

The play would have astounded Villon, and his friends, too. The famous—or infamous—Abbess Huguette du Hamel, with whom Villon passed time when he left Paris after the death of the priest Sermoise, appears as a waitress at the Pomme de Pin. A wistful girl, she is hopelessly in love with Villon. Thibaud d'Aussigny, the bishop who jailed Villon in Meung, is Grand Constable of France and a pro-Burgundian traitor. Villon's childhood friend, René de Montigny, is also a traitor. As scene one opens, Louis XI, disguised, enters the Pomme de Pin. McCarthy revives here a legend that Louis made a habit of such masquerades in order to keep a finger on the pulse of his people. Louis buys Villon a tankard of Beaune. His tongue loosened, Villon climbs atop a barrel to denounce the king's policies, and, in an impromptu ballade of McCarthy's creation, tells what he would do "if Villon were the King of France."

Next on stage is the traitorous Thibaud, looking for rabble who can be bribed to help him kidnap Louis and deliver him to the Burgundians. Then comes Catherine de Vaucelles. At her request Villon picks a quarrel with Thibaud, who has been pestering her. The two men duel, swords in one hand, lanterns in the other. Villon wounds Thibaud. Police guards arrive. Thibaud orders them to hang Villon from the nearest lamppost. Louis intervenes, orders Villon freed. The captain of the guard asks: "Who are you to interfere with the king's justice?'' Throwing off his disguise, Louis answers, "I am the king."

He has been impressed by Villon's ideas of what he would do for the kingdom, had he the authority. He gives him Thibaud's job as Grand Constable for a week and tells him to see how much he can accomplish. There is a catch, however. Unless in the course of that week he wins the hand of Catherine, he is to suffer the sentence Thibaud imposed. The action of the week's span which the play covers consists of the wooing of Catherine and the battle with the Burgundians who are massed at the gates of Paris. Catherine promises to marry Villon if he can defeat the Burgundians. She has not recognized in Louis' new Grand Constable the tavern brawler who rescued her from Thibaud. When Villon reveals his identity to her, she withdraws her promise.

The plot also includes a new conspiracy to kidnap the king which Villon discovers and exposes, although with the king out of the way he could have held on to his high office. In the last scene he returns from battle with the Burgundians, triumphant, to mount the gallows. Catherine repents her refusal, but too late; the king's deadline has passed. The people of Paris, however, are determined to prevent the death of their savior. They march angrily in the streets; the king fears insurrection. He is forced to revoke the death sentence, but exiles Villon from Paris. Catherine goes with him.

Although the Villon that McCarthy puts on stage is a

creature of pure imagination, living a far different life from the true Villon's, he lives it as one would expect Villon to do under the same circumstances. As Grand Constable, McCarthy's Villon is required to exercise justice. What he exercises is mercy. The pickpockets and prostitutes of Paris meet a presiding judge who knows what drove them to their trades and helps them to change their way of life. The Burgundians-at-the-gate situation gives full play to Villon's passion for France, and there are scenes with his mother which reflect the depths of understanding that enabled him to write her prayer. As one reviewer of a Boston, Massachusetts, performance of the play stated, "Mr. McCarthy has handled the rhyming rascal with a wide margin of poetic license, but only in order to make him more himself for the benefit of theater audiences."

In 1925 Brian Hooker and Rudolf Friml made McCarthy's play into an operetta with the title *The Vagabond King*. Like the drama from which it was adapted, *The Vagabond King* also became a movie. It had a long life on both stage and screen, with a succession of stars playing Villon, including the actor Dennis King and the singer Mario Lanza. The musical score has the richness of stained glass and the same kaleidoscopic impact. Whether the rousing chorus of Parisian rabble massing to defend Paris from the Burgundians, the fragile love songs of Villon and Catherine, the sales cries of the prostitutes, or the laments of Huguette— all the songs are remarkable for their power to evoke mood.

Like Debussy, Friml was fond of modulation. He used dissonance to break or change mood. He frequently inserted sliding scales of chromatics—that is, sequences using all the notes on the piano keyboard, both black and white. The wild air and the sense of hopelessness in Huguette's lament, a waltz, come from cascading chromatics, counterpointed by humming woodwinds and combined with crashing accents on alternate beats.

Heavy accenting also builds urgency in Villon's call to arms as his raggle-taggle army gathers to break the Burgundian siege of Paris. The music begins quietly enough, with a waspish plucking of violin strings. The stage begins to fill. The zizzing of strings loudens ominously. Villon bounds to a platform and addresses the assembly, the crowd murmuring in chorus behind his voice:

> "Ye beggars of Paris town,
> Ye lousy rabble of low degree—"

"Rabble of low degree," echoes the crowd.

> "We'll spare King Louis to keep his crown
> And save the city from Burgundy—"

Again the echo, louder this time: "From Burgundy."

> "We are good for nothing but to die,
> We can die for liberty!"

Villon urges. Then, as his voice gains power, the accenting begins:

> "*Sons* of toil and danger,
>   *Will* you serve a stranger
>   And bow *down* to Burgundy?
> *Sons* of *shame* and sorrow,
>   *Will* you cheer tomorrow
>   For the *crown* of Burgundy?
> *Forward! Forward! Swords* against the foe!
> *Onward! Onward!* The lily banners go:
> *Sons* of France around us,
>   *Break* the chain that *bound* us—
>   And to *hell* with Burgundy!"

The murmur of the crowd rises along with the orchestra's violins. Drums beat as halberds, swords, and banners are lifted. Villon and the vagabonds form a column and are off.

In a contrasting mood are the tender duets, such as *Only a Rose I Give You* and *Borrow Tomorrow with Me Today,* which Catherine and Villon sing together. *Borrow Tomorrow,* and a solo, *Love Me Tonight,* are inspired by Villon's warnings of the brevity of youth, in his *Ballade to His Beloved.* The duets, often harp-rippled, are close to rounds—that is, one voice comes in on the melody a few beats after the other, with the delay between the two calculated to produce harmony. Unlike rounds, however,

Friml's duets bring the voices together again toward the end. In solos, such as a lovely nocturne sung by Villon, the composer produces a similar effect by using a chorus to hum the melody a few beats behind the voice of the soloist.

Throughout the operetta, the violin is the most prominent instrument in the orchestral accompaniment. Friml makes it imitate sounds usually created by other instruments. With the deepest of notes he produces a drum roll; with the highest, the plaintive call of a horn. Other parts of the orchestra he uses to make rapid changes in pace. *Love for Sale* begins with wailing violins and voices. Their burden is reminiscent of *Les Regrets de la Belle Heaulmière*, by which the song is inspired. Suddenly cymbals clash. There is a tremulo of woodwinds. The dirge turns into a dance. Four times during the song, using the same notes but different instruments and different tempos, Friml alternates between the mournful and the gay, the funereal and the sprightly, much as Villon himself did in the verses comparing la Belle Heaulmière's past and present.

Since the staging of *The Vagabond King*, many writers have sought to re-create Villon, or to explain his work. Students at the University of Paris have dramatized his life for their own entertainment. A sensitive study of his life and poetry was published by the English poet, Richard Aldington. There have been several French novels about him, including one by Francis Carco, a popular poet and fiction writer of the first half of the twentieth century. But it was left for the American poet-novelist Babette Deutsch to write the story which, of all the modern interpretations of Villon, stays closest to what he told us of himself. *Rogue's Legacy,* the title of Miss Deutsch's tale, begins with the death of the priest Sermoise and follows the poet to the day of his disappearance. It includes scenes at the court of Charles d'Orléans, scenes with Paris pals, scenes in jail, and scenes on the highroad. The prose is interspersed with graceful translations of some of the ballades.

As numerous as speculations about Villon's life are the translations and editions of his poetry. No century has elapsed since his own without the publication of some version—and, except for the seventeenth and eighteenth centuries, several versions—of his work. He seems to have a word for every age.

The reason why has perhaps been best explained by a great modern Russian writer, Ilya Ehrenburg. In the preface to his Russian translation of Villon's poetry, he said: "While writers of the Middle Ages have left us lives of saints, Villon has given us the life of a man on this earth." Certainly, much of Villon's writing speaks directly to us living today on a continent undiscovered in Villon's time. The urban crime and poverty, the social and economic inequalities of which he wrote are the headlines of this morning's newspaper. But Villon's magnetism goes deeper than headlines. He did more than observe events. As Ehrenburg suggests, he *lived* them. And he describes his involvement with breath-taking honesty. This honesty has been strong stuff for some, like Robert Louis Stevenson; it has been over-glamorized by others—McCarthy, perhaps; but clearer than the voices of either critic or devotee, Villon's own verses speak for themselves across the centuries. He may have been a stranger in his own land; he is no stranger in ours.

Bibliography

Starred listings indicate materials that will interest readers who are loath to leave Villon at the end of this book. The starred collection of his poetry, edited by André Mary, is in relatively modern French and comes in paperback. (This collection and the one containing H. De Vere Stacpoole's translations are the sources of the French text quoted in this volume.) The Mary edition contains a concise biography and a detailed, indexed appendix explaining all Villon's references to people, places, history, legend, and Biblical lore. For anyone reading Villon for the first time, this edition is a compact, comprehensive guide.

Adams, Leónie, Introduction in the Swinburne collection of *Lyrics*. Croton Falls, N.Y., Spiral Press, 1933.

Aldington, Richard, *François Villon Criterion,* Vol. III, No. 2. London, April 1925.

*Anderson, Robert Gordon, *Villon*. Philadelphia, Lippincott, 1927.

Bedier, Joseph, and Hazard, Paul, *Histoire de la Littérature Française*. Paris, Larousse, 1923.

Carco, Francis, "Villon, Expliqué par Lui-même," *Revue de France*, Année 11, Tome 3. Paris, 1931.

*Champion, Pierre, *François Villon: Sa Vie et Son Temps*. Paris, Librairie Honoré Champion, 1933. 2nd ed.

*————, "La Cité au Temps de François Villon," *Revue de Paris,* v. 4, 1913.

*Charpier, Jacques, *Un Tableau Synoptique de la Vie et des Evénements Artistiques, Littéraires et Historiques du XV Siècle.* Paris, P. Soghers, 1958.

Cheney, Edward F., *François Villon at St. Benoît.* John Rylands Library (Manchester) Bull., v. 28, 1944.

Ciaramello, Michele, *A Short History of English Literature.* N.Y., Thomas Crowell, 1967.

Debussy, Claude, *Trois Ballades de François Villon.* Paris, Durand et Cie., 1910 (sheet music).

*Deutsch, Babette, *Rogue's Legacy.* N.Y., Coward-McCann, 1942.

Du Boulay, *Histoire de l'Université de Paris.* Paris, P. Champion, 1912.

*Erskine, John, *The Brief Hour of François Villon.* Indianapolis, Bobbs-Merrill, 1937.

Foulet, Lucien, *Villon et Charles d'Orléans,* in *Medieval Studies in Memory of Gertrude Schoepperle.* Paris, Librairie Honoré Champion, 1927.

————, *Villon et la Scolastique,* Romania, Tome 65, 1939.

————, *Villon et le Duc de Bourbon,* in *Mélanges de Philologie et d'Histoire,* 1927.

*Friml, Rudolf (with Brian Hooker and W. H. Post), *The Vagabond King.* Record, starring Mario Lanza. Victor Records, LSC-2509.

La Mure, E., *Histoire des Ducs de Bourbon.* Paris, Gaston, 1868.

Livre Noir du Châtelet, 1427 Archives, ms. X²⁴ 25, Bibliothèque de Paris.

Longford, Elizabeth, *Queen Victoria*. N.Y., Harper & Row, 1964.

Longnon, Auguste, *Oeuvres Complètes de Villon, d'Après les Manuscrits et les plus Anciennes Editions*. Paris, Longnon, 1892. *Avec les Observations de Gaston Paris,* 1932.

————, *L'Etude Biographique d'Après les Documents Inédits, Conservés aux Archives Nationales.*

McCarthy, Justin Huntly, *If I Were King*. N.Y., Grosset & Dunlap, 1929.

————, *Needles and Pins*. N.Y., Harper, 1907.

————, "The Tale of François Villon," *Theatre,* Vol. I, No. 10 (Dec. 1901).

Michel, François, and Fournier, Édouard, *Histoire des Hostelleries et Cabarets*. Paris, Piper, 1902.

*Moorehead, George, *The Story of François Villon*. N.Y., S. S. Ogilvie, 1901.

Orléans, Charles d', *Manuscrits des Poésies (Reproduits en Photocopie par la Société des Anciens Textes)*. Paris, 1910.

Paris, H., *Le Jargon de François Villon*. Paris, Daragon, 1909.

Phillips, C. H., *The Symbolists and Debussy,* Humberside, v. III, No. 3 (Oct. 1930).

Plattard, M. J., *Le Poète François Villon en Poitou*. Poitiers, Société des Antiquités de l'Ouest, 1914.

Port, Celestin, *Inventaire Analytique des Archives Anciennes de la Mairie d'Angers*. Un. d'Angers, 1861.

Réunion d'Arrêts Relatifs Surtout aux Conflits des Justices Ecclésiastiques et Royales, de la Fin du XIVe Siècle et du Premiers Tiers du XVe Siècle. Bibliothèque National, Lat. 12811, Fol. 29.

Robinson, James Harvey, *The Ordeal of Civilization*. N.Y., Harper, 1926.

Robinson Locke Collection of Theatre Reviews. New York Public Library.

Schwob, Marcel, *François Villon, Rédactions et Notes*. Paris, Champion, 1912.

————, *Oeuvres Complètes de François Villon*. Paris, Longnon, 1903.

Stabler, Jordan Herbert, *The Jargon of Master François Villon*. Cambridge, Riverside, 1918.

Stacpoole, H. De Vere, *François Villon: His Life and Times*. London, Hutchinson, 1916.

*Stevenson, Robert Louis, *A Lodging for the Night*. N.Y., Grolier, 1902.

————, *Familiar Studies of Men and Books*. London, Mosher, 1902.

————, *François Villon*. London, Mosher, 1911.

————, *Poems of François Villon*. London, Luce, 1917.

Tientôt, Yvonne, *Debussy, l'Homme, Son Oeuvre, Son Milieu*. Paris, O. D'estrade-Guerra, Henri Lemoine et Cie., 1962.

Troche, M., "Notice Historique sur l'Ancienne Eglise Collégiale et Paroissale de St. Benoît," in *Revue Archéologique,* Tome IV, 1847.

Tuetly, A., *Testaments Enregistrés au Parlement de Paris.* Un. of Paris, 1889.

Villon, François. *The Book of François Villon: The Little Testament and Ballads.* Translated by Algernon Charles Swinburne, Dante Gabriel Rossetti, and John Payne. Boston, International Pocket Library, 1931.

————, *Oeuvres,* edition de André Mary. Paris, Garnier Frères, 1962.

————, *The Poems of François Villon.* Translated by H. De Vere Stacpoole. London, Hutchinson.

Vitu, Auguste, *Le Jargon et Jobelin.* Paris, P. Ollendorf, 1889.

Index